STARTER GUIDES

COLOUR

and Creativity

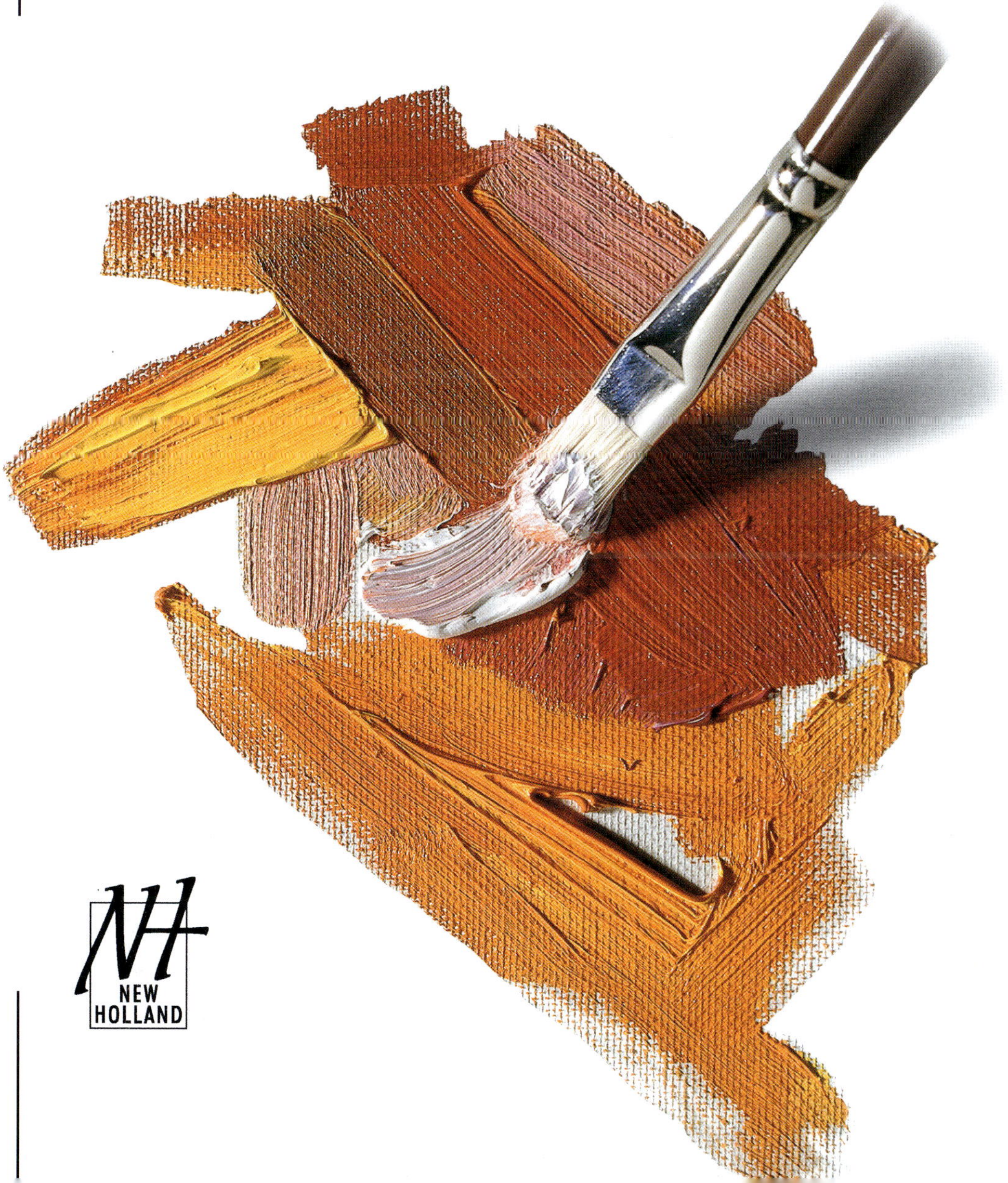

NEW HOLLAND

First published in the UK in 2006 by
New Holland Publishers (UK) Ltd
London • Cape Town • Sydney • Auckland
www.newhollandpublishers.com

Garfield House, 86–88 Edgware Road, London W2 2EA

80 McKenzie Street, Cape Town 8001, South Africa

Level 1, Unit 4, 14 Aquatic Drive, Frenchs Forest, NSW 2086, Australia

218 Lake Road, Northcote, Auckland, New Zealand

Original title of the book in Spanish:
GUIAS PARA PRINCIPIANTES: COLOR Y CREATIVIDAD

Published by Parramon Ediciones, S. A., Barcelona, Spain

ISBN 1 84537 515 7

10 9 8 7 6 5 4 3 2 1

Authors: Parramon Editorial
Text: Gabriel Martín Roig
Exercises: Gabriel Martín Roig and Óscar Sanchís
Photograhy: Nos & Soto

English translation by Michael Brunelle and Beatriz Cortabarría

Printed in Spain

CONTENTS

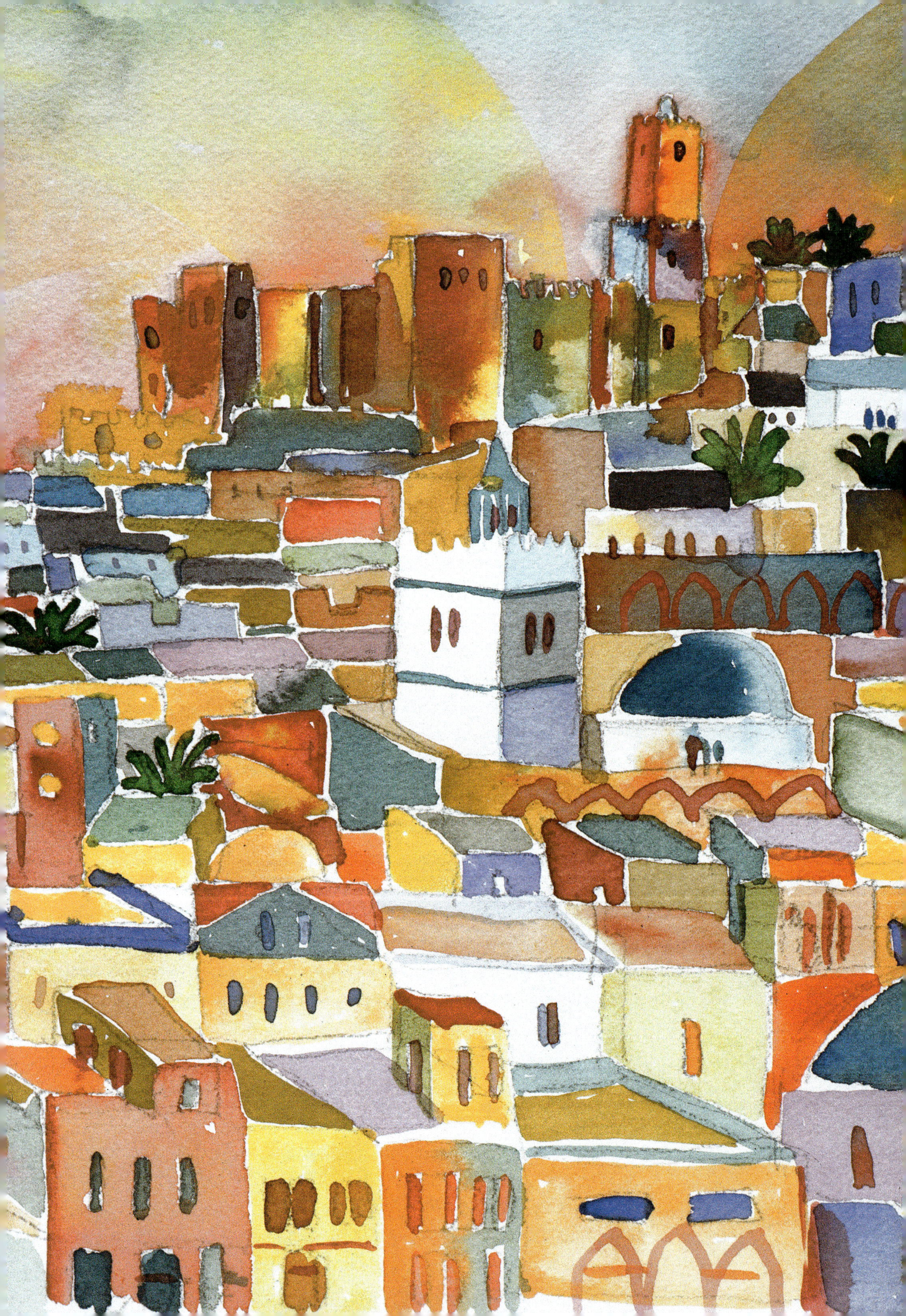

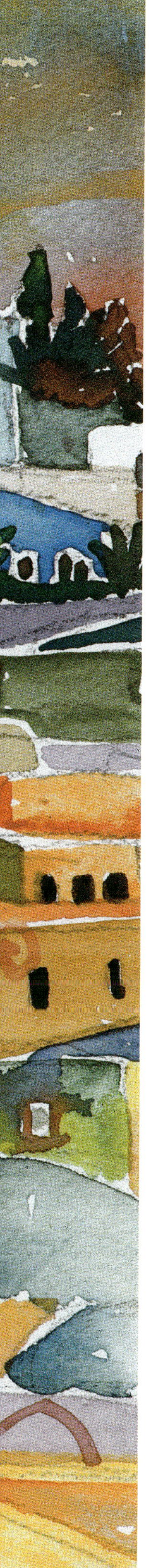

Introduction

COLOUR *and* FORM

When a person creates a painting, many different aspects contribute to his or her interpretation of the subject; colour, however, is the artist's most effective tool for creating contrasts and the most ideal vehicle for moving the viewer. The use of colour on the surface of the painting provides visual information and is a very powerful design element, a basic attribute of the painting, just like composition and form. Colour is essential in helping us capture information from the infinite number of visual images and finding a way to interpret it.

Another important aspect of colour is its emotive content, its ability to stimulate our senses. Colour can be used to suggest and accentuate the character of a painting, creating an emotional response in the mind of the viewer. Colour affects our emotions much more than we think, and it can cause any state, from delight to desperation, from torment to uneasiness, from serenity to excitement. It can be subtle, sensual or spectacular.

When observing paintings, it becomes obvious that there are many ways to interpret and manipulate the chromatic effects. In this book we will show you some techniques for correctly using the interactions of colours to overcome specific visual challenges, for example, how to create natural descriptive colours and how to use the expressive qualities of colour to create interesting images with a personal style. We also cover practical and aesthetic considerations regarding the use of colour in each medium, based on examples, step-by-step exercises and a helpful notebook.

Becoming familiar with the potential of colour requires firsthand experience like that provided by this book. The rest depends on you – on your willingness to practise and to see colour as a protagonist, a most basic constructive element of painting.

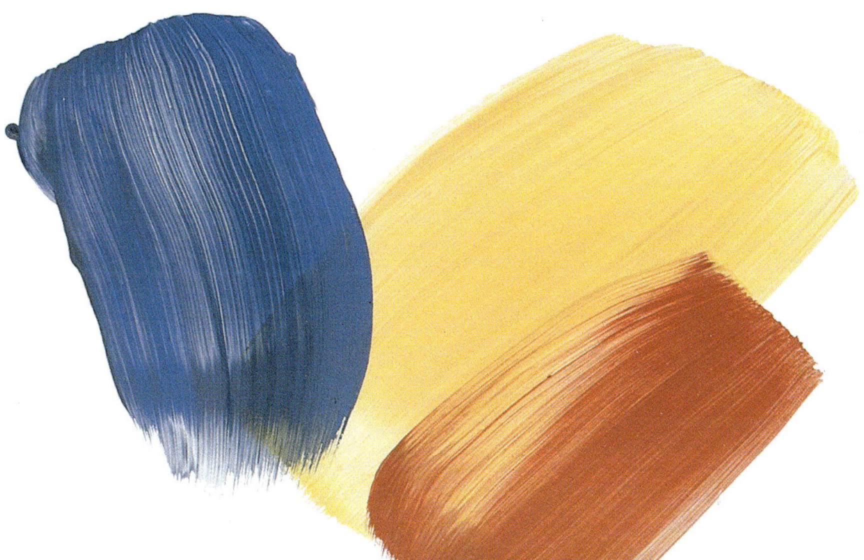

PERCEPTION *and*

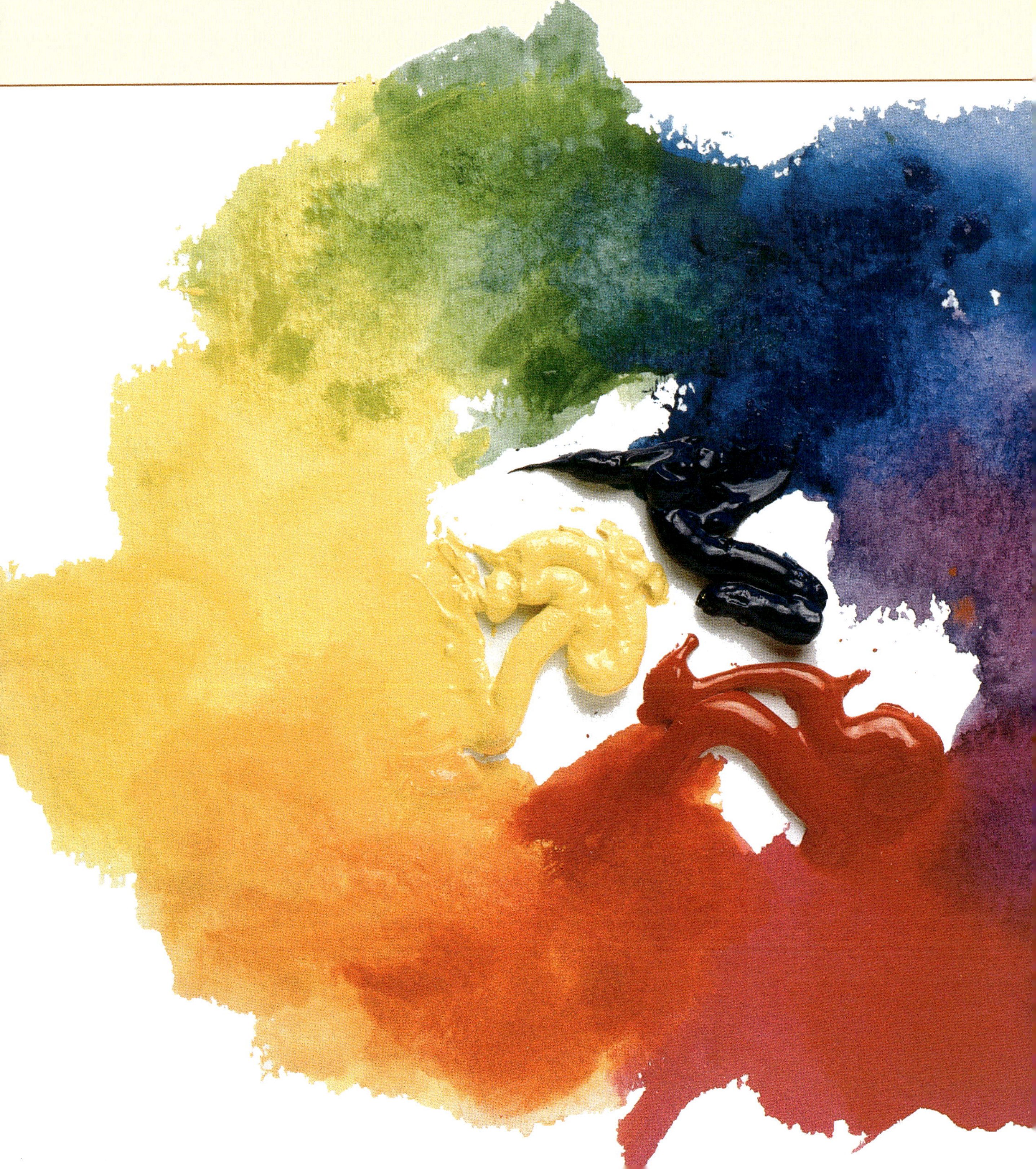

INTERPRETATION

PERCEPTION *and* INTERPRETATION

Colour is one of the most personal and expressive elements of a painting. Using it skillfully will give any subject a distinctive character or feeling. Learning to appreciate colours and interact with them is the first step in creating a successful work of art. When working with colours, explore their characteristics and carefully observe how they modify each other, how they describe form and how they infuse the painting with expression. At first it will be difficult to use colour correctly, and you might even make a few mistakes; however, there are some guidelines, which we cover in this chapter, that will help you achieve the best results.

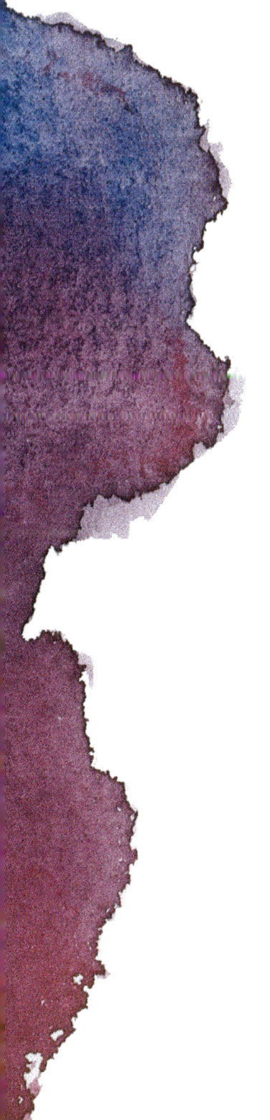

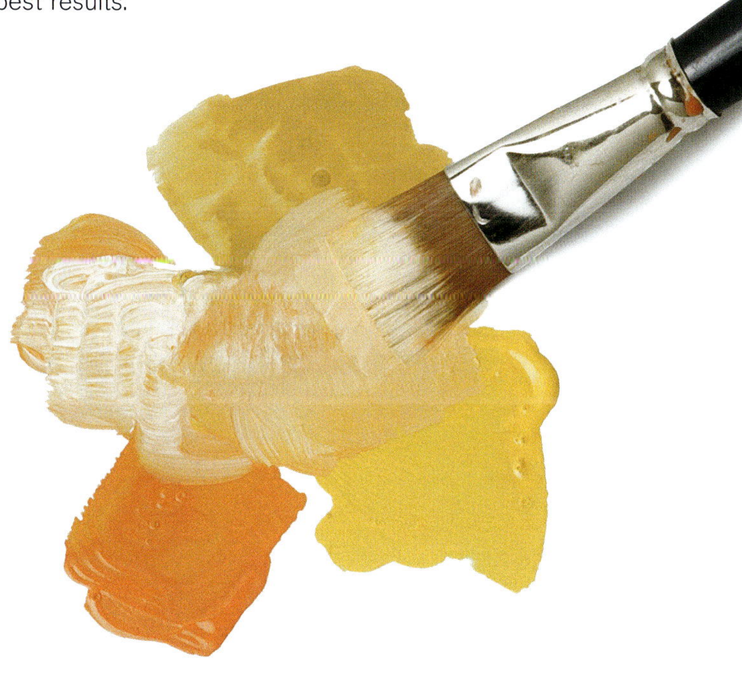

The Colour WHEEL

It may be surprising to learn that it is often difficult for us to recognize the colours of an actual subject. To learn to identify and classify them, it is necessary to understand how they are distributed – to see their locations on the colour wheel, to understand how they relate to each other and to learn how to make use of these relationships.

To understand how the colour wheel is constructed, we can simply imagine a circle formed by three fans showing the three primary colours: yellow, magenta and cyan blue.

A Diagram of the Primary Colours

The colour wheel is a diagram of colours that can be organized in different ways, but the colour relationships it describes are standardized. It is based on the idea that pure colours are derived from the three primaries: magenta, yellow and cyan blue. They are defined as primaries because they cannot be created by combining other colours. This means that the basic primary colours are completely autonomous and have no chromatic similarity to any other colour.

OBTAINING SECONDARY COLOURS

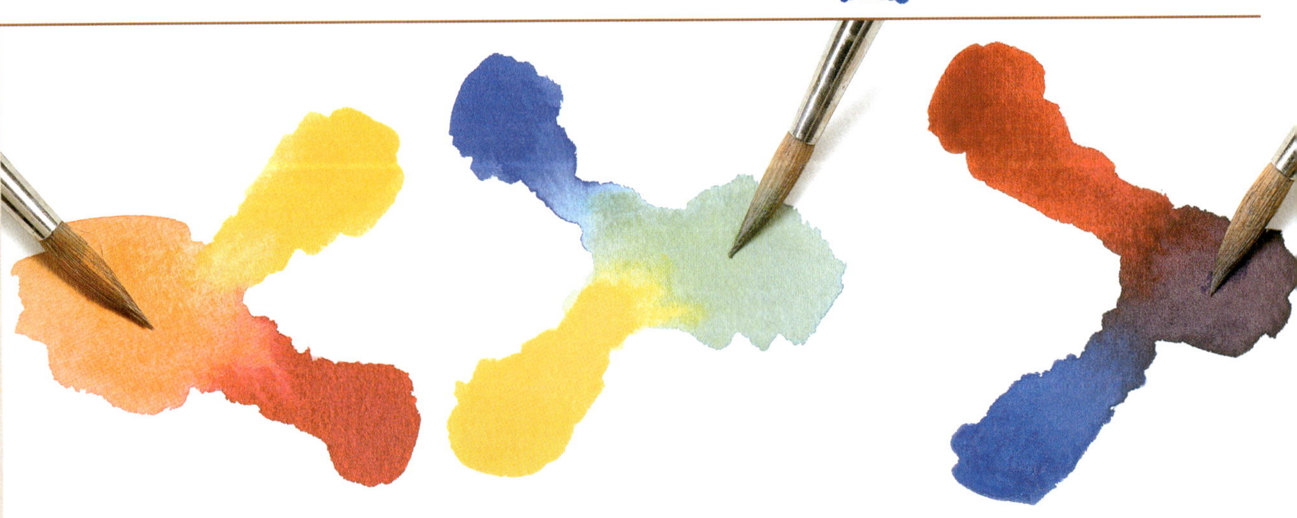

We mix two primaries together to make secondary colours. If we wish to make orange, we must mix equal portions of magenta and yellow.

We mix equal parts of yellow and cyan blue to make green.

Violet is made by mixing the last two primary colours, cyan blue and magenta.

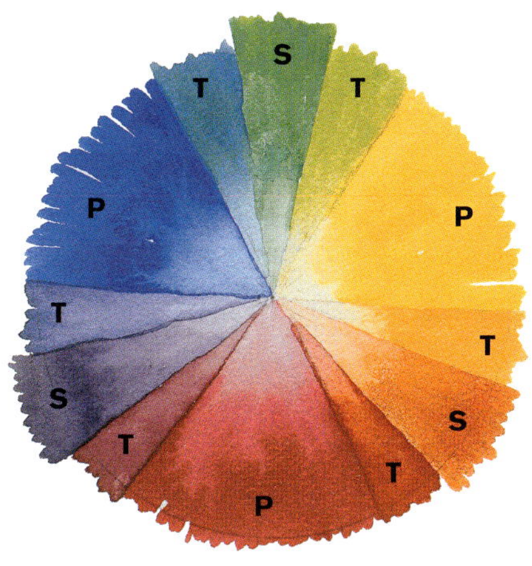

*Between the three primary colours (**P**) we can place the secondary colours (**S**), which result from mixing the primaries in equal proportions, and the tertiary colours (**T**), which result from mixing the same colours in unequal proportions.*

Tip

When two or more colours from the colour circle are mixed, they lose strength; a colour resulting from a mixture is rarely as intense as its component colours.

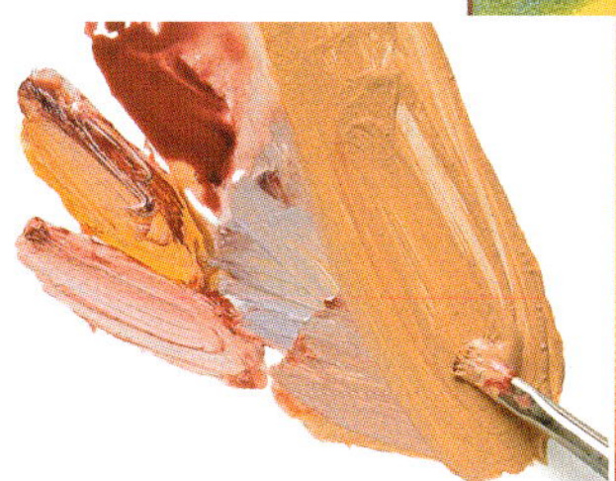

Inserting the Secondary and Tertiary Colours

We insert the colour that is made from each pair of primary colours between them all around the colour wheel. Thus, the wheel includes the primary and secondary colours. The tertiary colours can be included by placing them between each pair of colours from which they are mixed. The colours that are opposite each other on the colour wheel are markedly different from each other and are called complementary colours.

Analyzing Colours

It is possible to analyze the colours of a subject by using a colour wheel and small amounts of paint to help identify and harmonize the colours that we see. If the colours are not well defined, like browns, greys and neutrals, we must find the chromatic influences: a greenish brown, or a reddish brown, according to what blends best with the rest of the colours.

Theory and Practice

In actual painting, the primary colours like cyan blue and magenta are rarely used, so a similar paint must be chosen to represent the pure colour. Different blues are usually used, like ultramarine and Prussian; vermilion or cadmium red are used in place of magenta. However, the substitutions do not invalidate the colour theory. On the contrary, this should lead you to become conscious of the mechanics of colour implicit in your work.

In practice, ultramarine blue and cadmium red or similar colours are usually substituted for cyan blue and magenta.

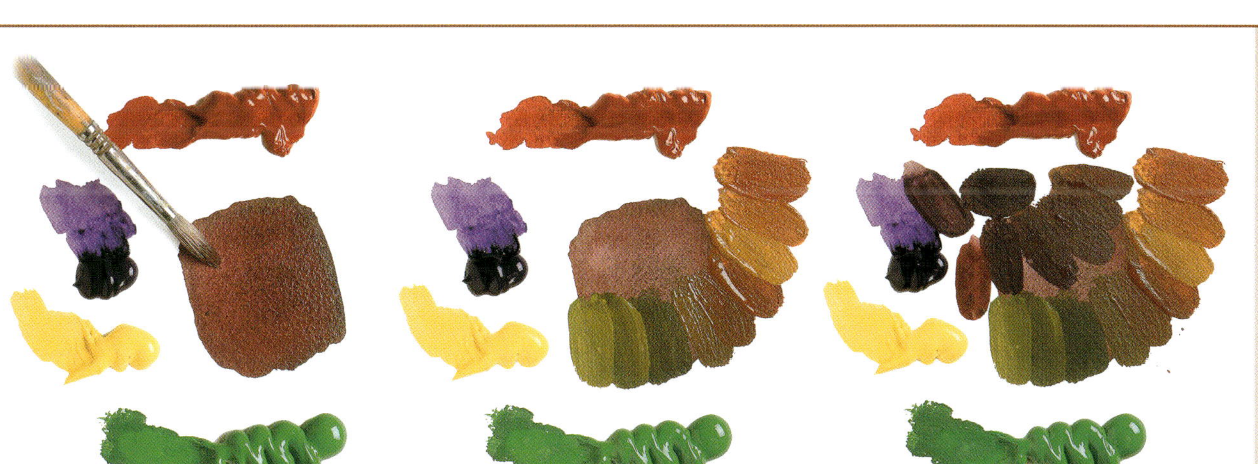

The tertiary colours are mixtures of two primaries in unequal quantities, or of a tertiary and a secondary; for example, with magenta (primary) and green (secondary) we make brown.

Starting with the brown base we develop a range of lighter browns by mixing the initial colour with different amounts of yellow.

We enlarge the range of browns by darkening the initial brown with different proportions of violet, to which we can add a dab of magenta to redden the final colour.

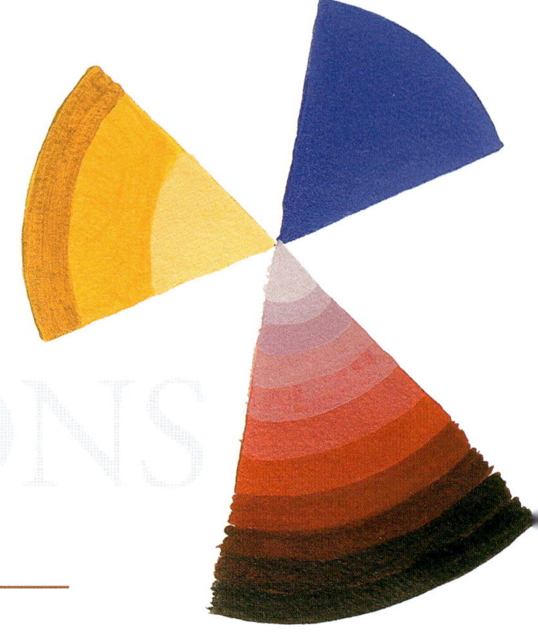

GRADATIONS *of* COLOUR

It is very important to understand the gradations of saturation, tone and value of colours to model a form, locate the placement of colours and express the volume. Correct differentiation between the various gradations of the same colour gives an immediate view of the layout and content of the painting.

The range of values of a colour consists of lightening the colour with white or darkening it with black. This will create scales like the cadmium red and the yellow seen here.

The Intensity of a Colour

The amount of saturation or intensity of a colour refers to its strength and brightness. A colour is at its peak saturation when it is pure, without the addition of black or white, preserving the inherent strength of the original pigment.

The Difference Between Tone and Value

The terminology that is used when speaking about colour consists of many imprecise and contradictory words. To avoid confusion, we will explain what we mean by each concept. Tone is an attribute of colour that relates to the amount of movement of this colour toward that of its neighboring colour. For example, a yellow can have a green or an orange tone. Value is the transition that a colour makes from light to dark, that is, each grade of variation that a colour will go through before becoming white or black. Therefore, when we mix a colour with black or white we change its value but not its tone.

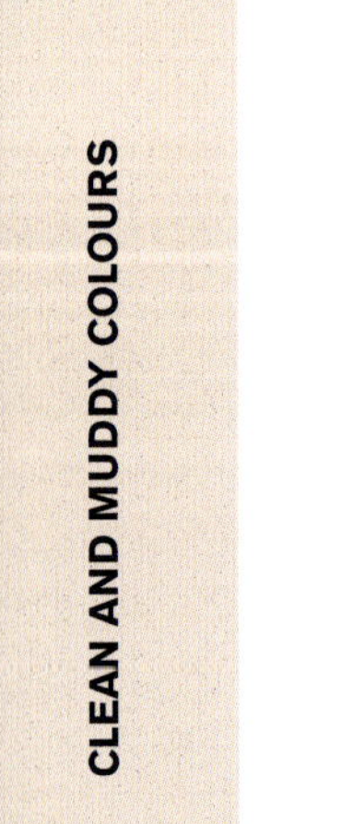

CLEAN AND MUDDY COLOURS

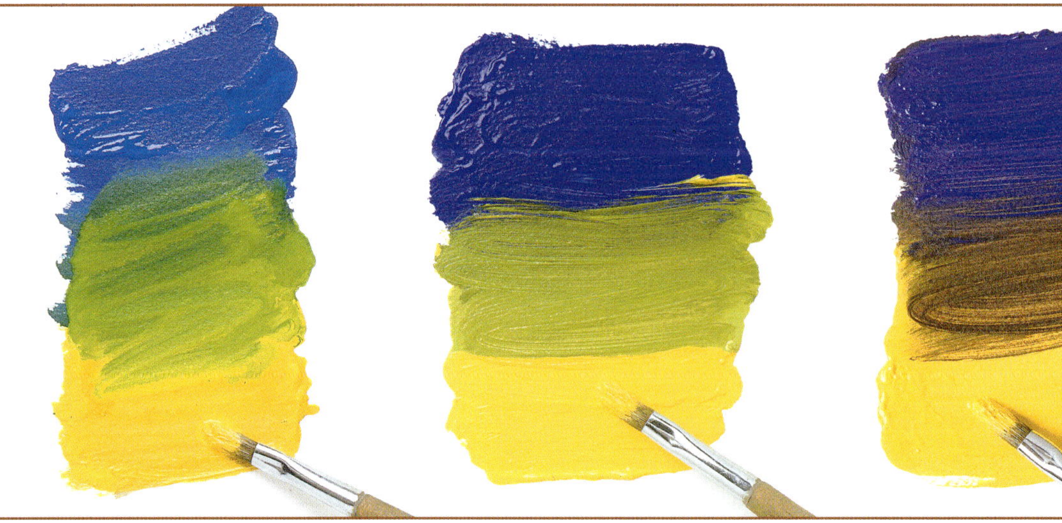

Mixing cadmium yellow with different blues will give us different results. Yellow mixed with cyan blue will give us a clean and bright green.

The same yellow mixed with dark cobalt blue; here the resulting green still seems quite clean. Thus, cobalt blue and yellow do not make a very muddy mixture.

Finally, we mix the cadmium yellow with dark ultramarine blue. The result is very muddy. Instead of reviving the green, the ultramarine blue turns the colour mixture brown.

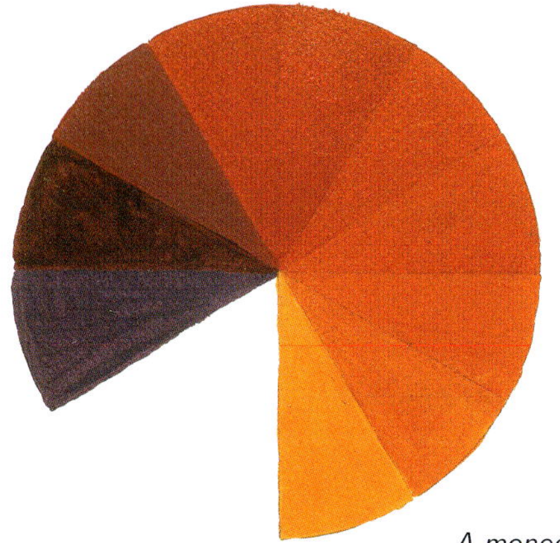

Here is a range of different red tones. Tone refers to the variations that a colour can produce when mixed with its neighboring colours on the colour wheel.

Tip

Colours of different tones that have the same value do not contrast with each other. They tend to optically blend with each other along their edges, causing the line that separates them to disappear.

A monochromatic work does not necessarily have to be black and white; greys and blues are often included in the mixture.

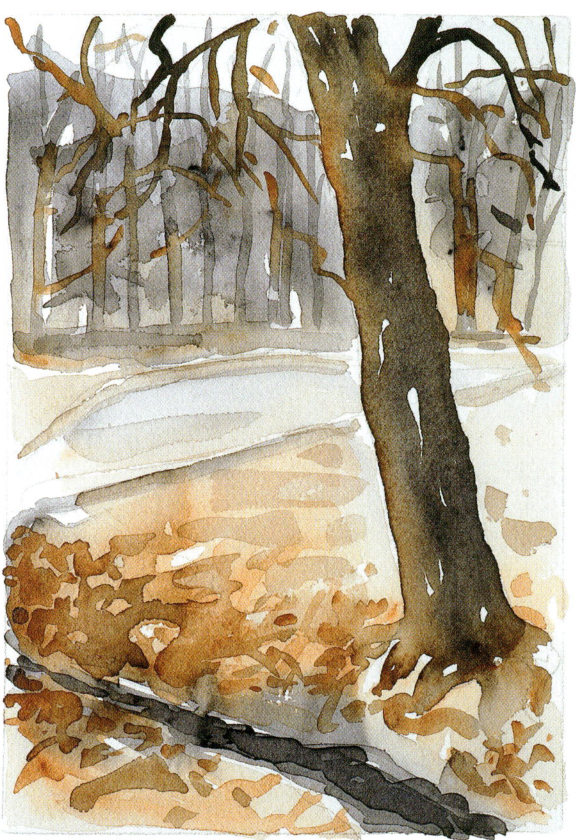

Monochromatic Scheme

A monochromatic scheme allows us to place full attention on the changes in value and the relationships between the forms on the picture planes. When painting a monochromatic subject, more than just a single colour can be used; black and white are often added to create variations in colour and saturation and thus avoid monotony. Some artists frequently break with the inherent unity of a monochromatic scheme by using neutral colours (greys and browns).

Analogous Values

One way of harmonizing a painting in a monochromatic manner is by beginning with an analogous colour scheme that uses several values that are adjacent on the colour wheel. Wide use of analogous colours can include three or four adjacent shades with many variations in value.

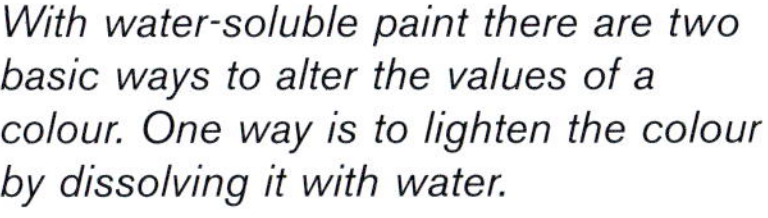

With water-soluble paint there are two basic ways to alter the values of a colour. One way is to lighten the colour by dissolving it with water.

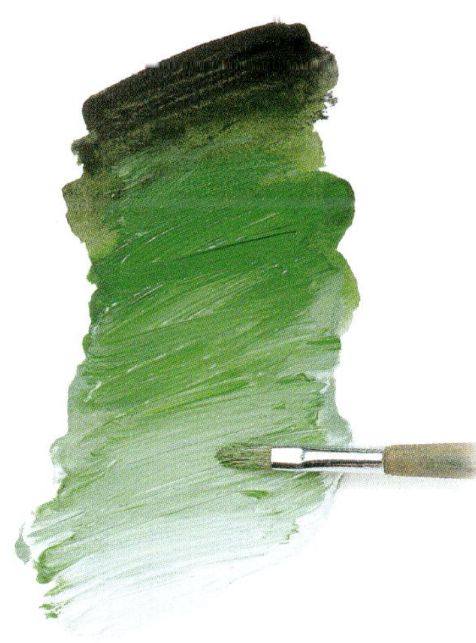

The second way of creating a graduated value scale is by adding black or white to the green, according to whether we want to lighten or darken the colour.

The last gradation is tonal, taking a colour toward another adjacent one on the colour wheel. In the centre of the gradation, the green clearly shows bluish tones.

FORM *Through* COLOUR

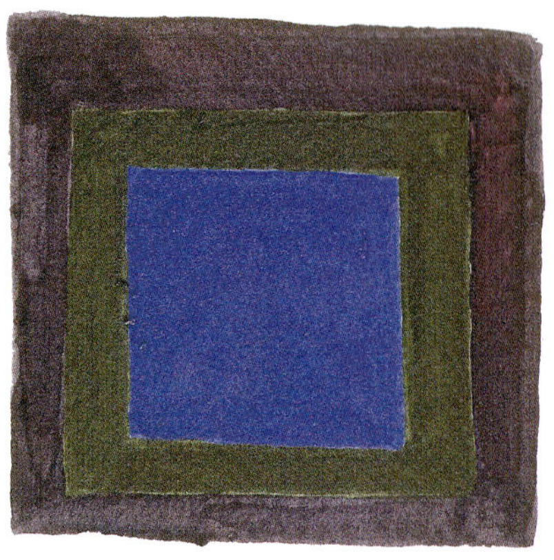

Working with colours that have the same tone and that are near each other on the colour wheel is not enough to differentiate the edges, since the contrast between them is not very strong and the outlines tend to run together.

The intensity and distribution of the colours in a painting usually determine the forms of the subject and give an immediate view of the composition. Defining the form based on colour requires simplifying what we see and making use of the juxtaposition of colours to define the outlines of the objects.

Outlining Forms

If we want to emphasize a form, we should contrast two colours that are far apart on the colour wheel and that are of different values, with different levels of luminosity. It is very effective to create forms by contrasting warm and cool, light and dark, complementary and saturated, and neutral colours. A strong contrast can be created between the object and the background, an effect that lasts even if we paint a blended, broken or linear outline.

Decorated Surfaces

Allowing a patterned background to completely invade the painting will create a striking, abstract and sometimes confusing effect. When placing decorative objects in the background, we should clarify the forms and the colours of the painting to stop the two planes from becoming confused. To keep a background pattern and an object from blending together, contrast should be created using a range of values and complementary colours.

EMPHASIZING AN OBJECT AGAINST A BACKGROUND

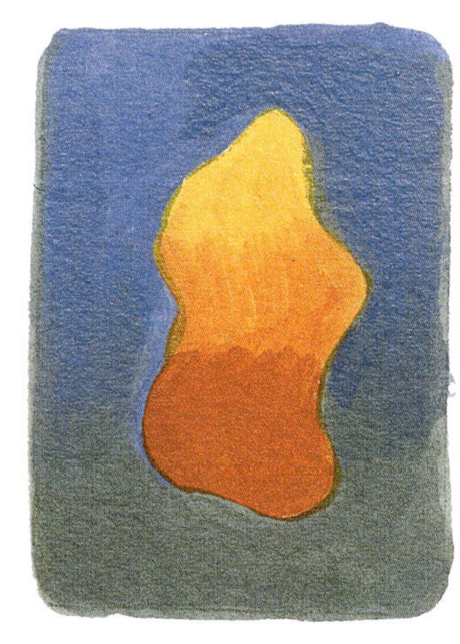

In this type of contrast, the near objects are painted in warm colours like yellow and red, while the background is a cool blue.

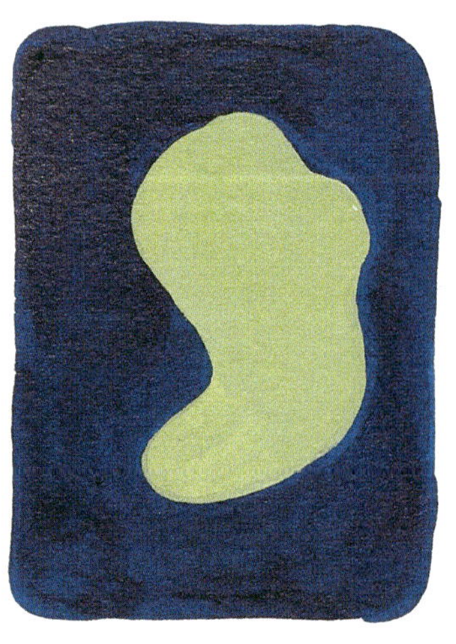

Using a single range of colour, a form painted with very light colours stands out against a background covered with very dark colours.

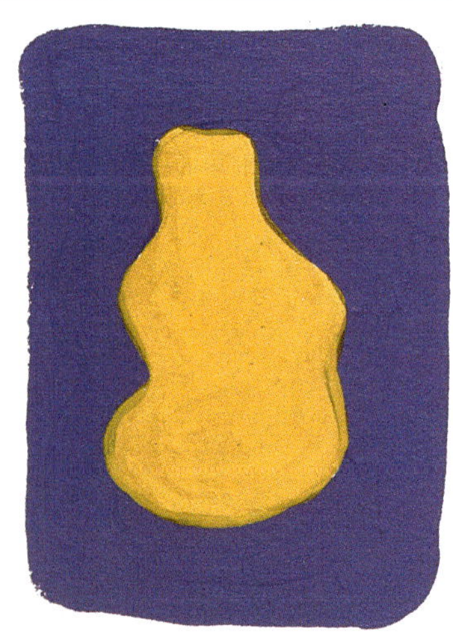

Two complementary colours are used to achieve the maximum amount of contrast. In this case, a yellow form clearly stands out against a violet background.

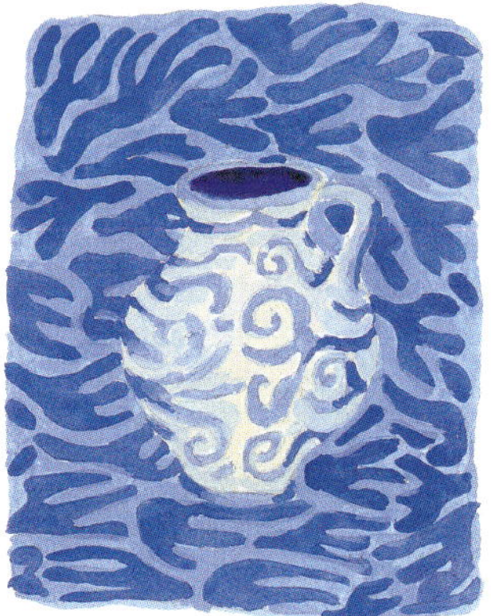

Two decorated surfaces (object and background), with similar designs and colours, tend to be confusing when put together.

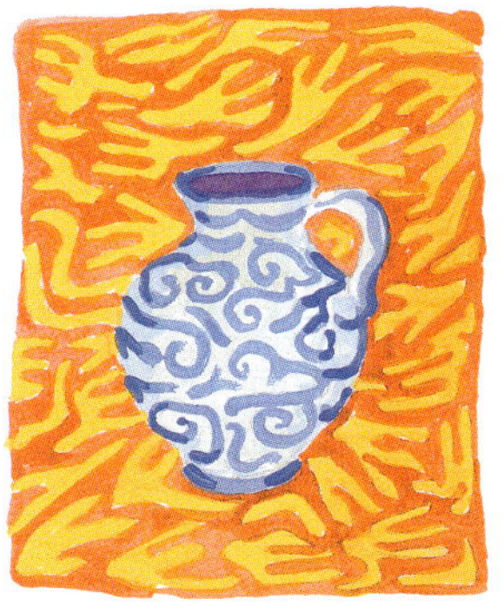

Tip

The use of colour is essential for identifying the subject when its colours are diffused and the outline is not sharp.

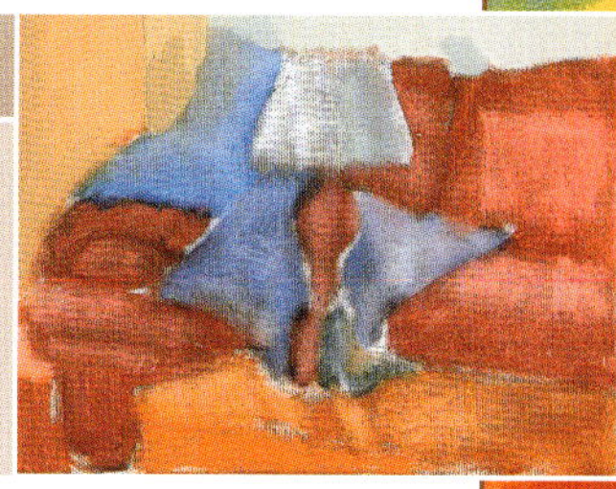

To make the object stand out clearly from the patterned background, the use of contrasting colour ranges for the object and the background is essential.

The Bezold Effect

It is possible to change the appearance of a work by changing or substituting a single colour. This effect is usually achieved by replacing the colour that occupies a larger area with a different one. Not only is the colour modified, but different forms stand out in one version and blend into the other with the single chromatic alteration. In some cases it is even possible to alter the entire work by changing a colour, especially if it is a strong one.

Phantom Colours

Sometimes colours extend farther than their physical boundaries to tint larger neutral areas with their tones. In this illustration, the background is off-white, but the thin blue lines along the lines with dots influence the white background. The effect is more evident in the orange stripes. These phantom colours are easier to see when the lines have broken edges rather than being perfectly straight.

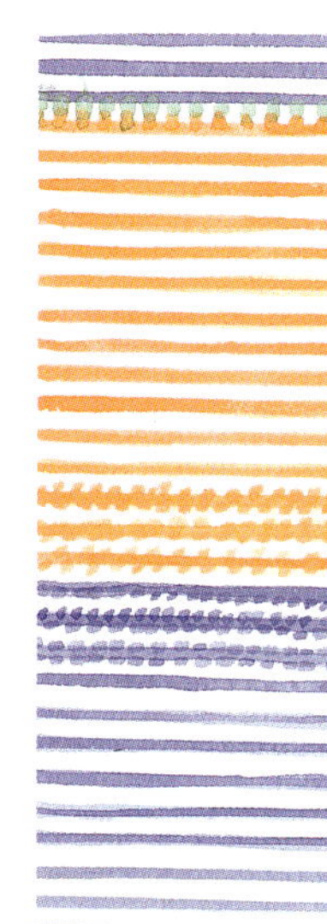

We can see here how the lines extend their influence to the off-white background. The stripes contaminate the background with their colour. Where the jagged orange and blue coincide, the background seems lighter and sparkling.

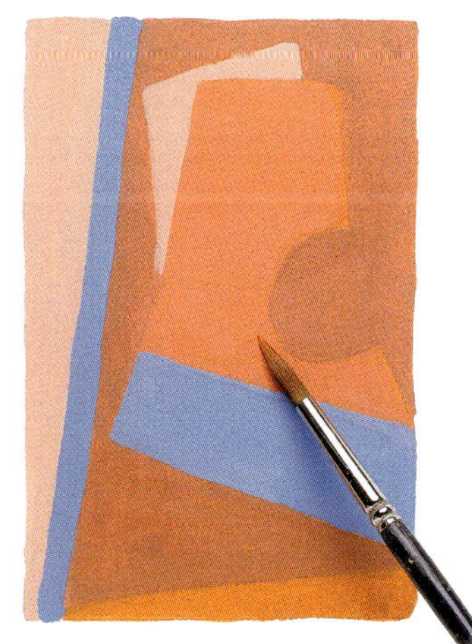

Here we paint an abstract design with orange, light raw sienna, blue and pink. The painting mostly consists of warm reddish tones, and the contrasting blue areas are emphasized.

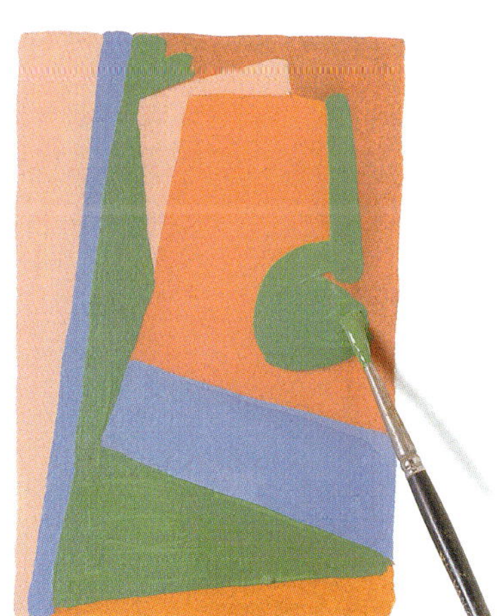

Changing a single colour in this design alters the appearance of the other colours. We begin covering the reddish sienna areas with a medium green.

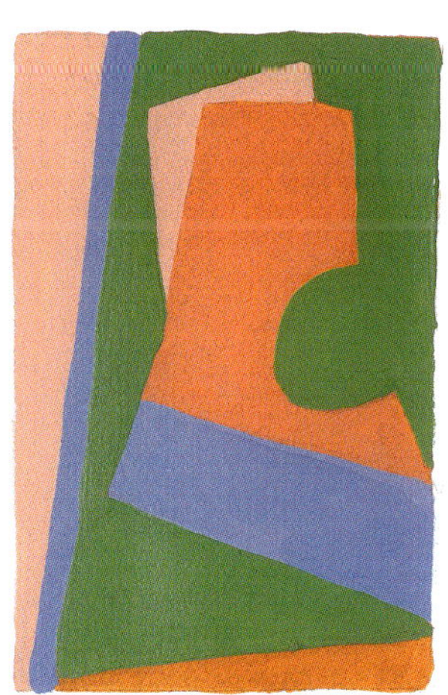

With the green colour, the blue that previously contrasted seems to now be more integrated. Not only is the colour modified, different forms stand out in one version and blend into the other.

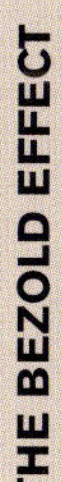

Contrasting Colour RANGES

Contrasting Colour RANGES

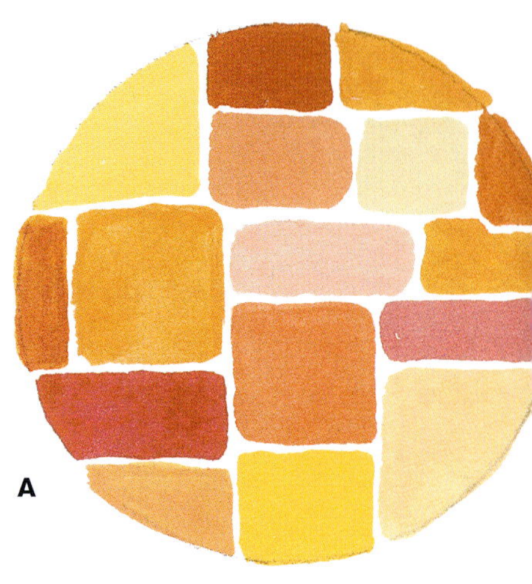

When we speak of colour ranges, we are referring to families of harmonic colours, colours that never clash with each other. If we juxtapose several ranges with different chromatic tendencies we are then dealing with contrasting ranges. For example, warm colours, like red, orange and yellow, placed next to a range of cool colours, like blues and greens, create the greatest possible contrast.

Colours in the same range are those that have colours in common.

Colours in the Same Range

Colours that are adjacent to each other on the colour wheel form part of the same range. The most closely related are a primary and a secondary containing that primary colour, through the intermediate tones created by mixing the two.

Warm and Cool Colour Ranges

We associate the colours of fire – reds, yellows and oranges – with warmth. Physiological research reveals that our bodies secrete more adrenaline under a red light. On the other hand, we associate blues and greens with the refreshing qualities of water and trees. Research shows that they slow down the heartbeat and relax the muscles. Thus the shades in the red and yellow area of the colour wheel are called warm, while those in the blue and green ranges are called cool.

WARM COLOURS ADVANCE

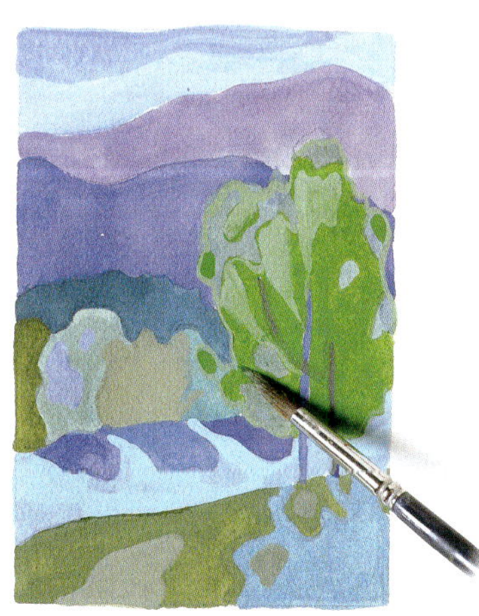

To understand how warm colours move toward the viewer, we first paint a sketch of a landscape with a range of cool colours.

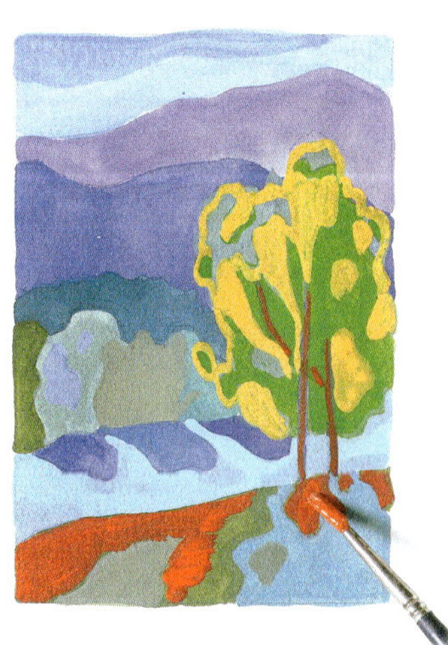

When this layer of colour has dried, we begin covering the ground and the tree in the foreground with warm colours that strongly contrast with the background colours.

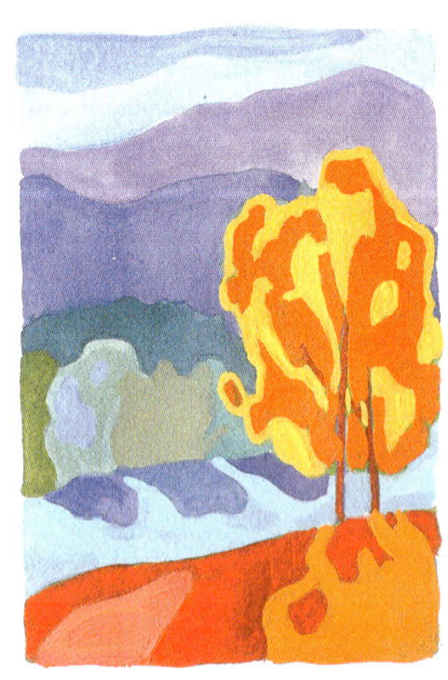

Now the foreground seems to be closer to the observer than the planes with cool colours. It is commonly believed that warm colours advance and that cool colours recede.

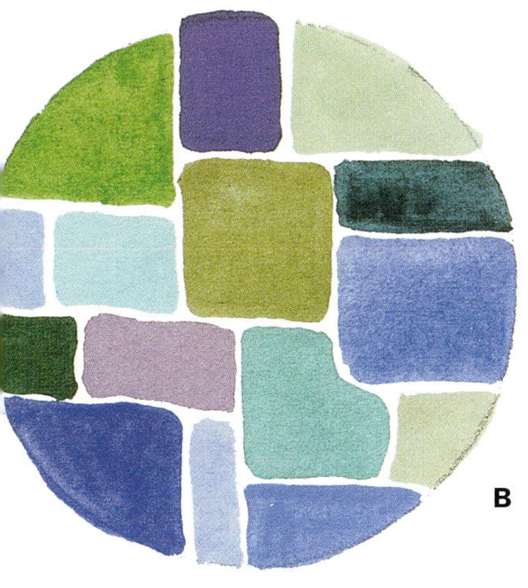
B

*(**A**) The warm colour range is mainly composed of reds, oranges and yellows.*

*(**B**) The cool colour range consists of greens, blues and their derivatives.*

Tip

A single colour can have the feeling of being either warm or cool, depending on the colour next to it. For example, green can feel warmer if it is compared to a dark violet, but it becomes cooler if it is next to a cadmium red.

Contrasting Ranges

In the physical sense, warm colours catch our attention more immediately than cool colours. They give the sensation that they advance toward the viewer from the surface of the painting, while the cool colours seem to recede. In the example below, all the colour circles are exactly the same size; optically, however, the yellow seems to be larger than the purple, which itself seems larger than the blue. Saturated colours like the bright yellow tend to seem larger than less saturated ones.

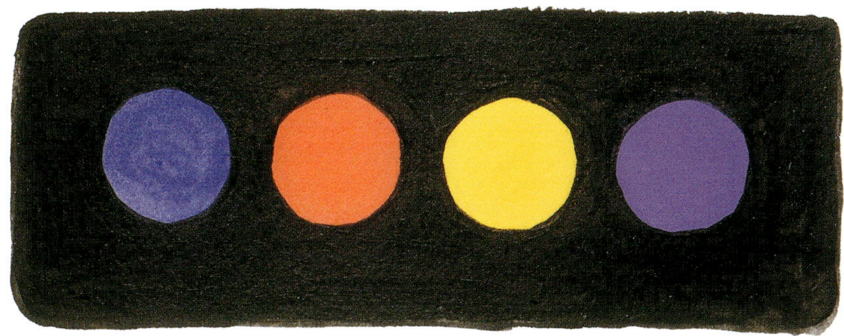

Cooling Warm Colours

Warm colours can be cooled by adding white, black or both at the same time (which is, of course, grey). The resulting colours continue to be warm, but have a lower "temperature". Another possibility is mixing them with the cool tone that is nearest to their position on the colour wheel; the result is a tone that is different from the original and cooler.

Although these four circles are of equal size, the two in the centre, painted with warm colours (red and yellow), seem to expand more than the blue and violet ones.

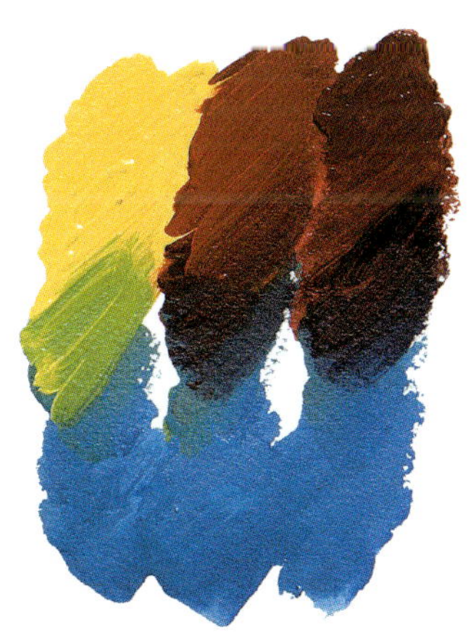

There are three basic ways to cool warm colours: the first way is to mix them with a colour from the cool range, in this case cyan blue.

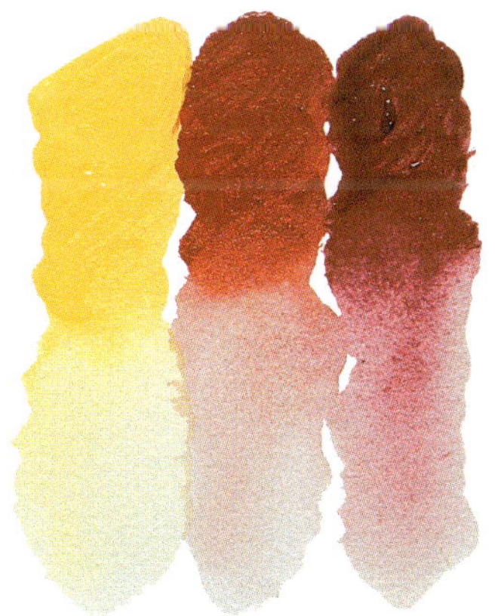

Another way is to dilute the colour with water so it will become less saturated, and consequently lose its brightness.

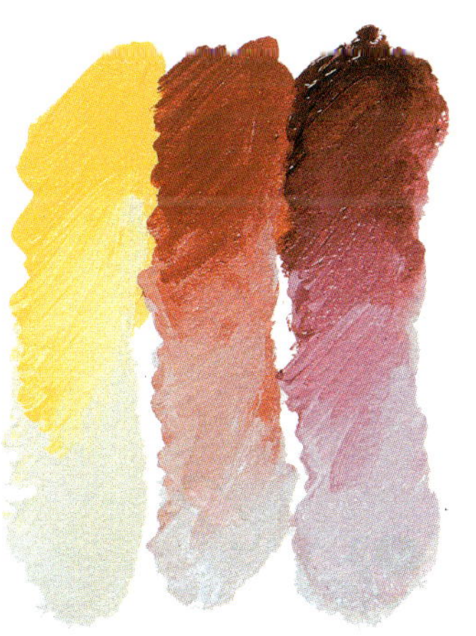

Finally, you can reduce the colour saturation by mixing it with white. White lightens and mitigates the brightness of many colours, cooling saturated warm colours.

Contrasting COMPLEMENTARY COLOURS

Contrasting COMPLEMENTARY COLOURS

The colours that are located directly opposite from each other on the colour wheel are called complementary colours. There are three main groups, each one consisting of a primary colour and a secondary colour: blue and orange, red and green and yellow and violet. Each of these pairs of opposite colours produces a particularly vivid and striking contrast.

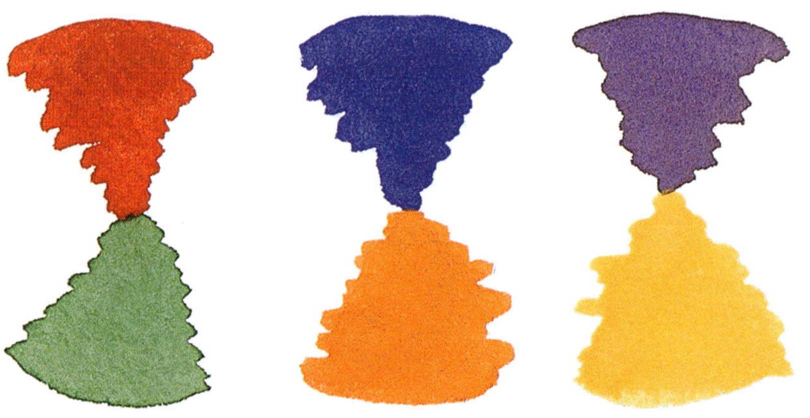

Contrasting Opposite Colours

The complementary relationships exist around the entire colour wheel. The juxtaposition of the complements can produce a very lively, sometimes even disturbing, visual sensation. Opposite tones compete in attracting our attention, and coloured areas next to each other will sometimes cause a physical effect, a sort of blinking or vibration. Some complementary colours are intensified when placed next to each other.

The complementary colours are opposite each other on the colour wheel: red is the complement of green, blue of orange and violet of yellow.

INTENSELY CONTRASTING COMPLEMENTARY COLOURS

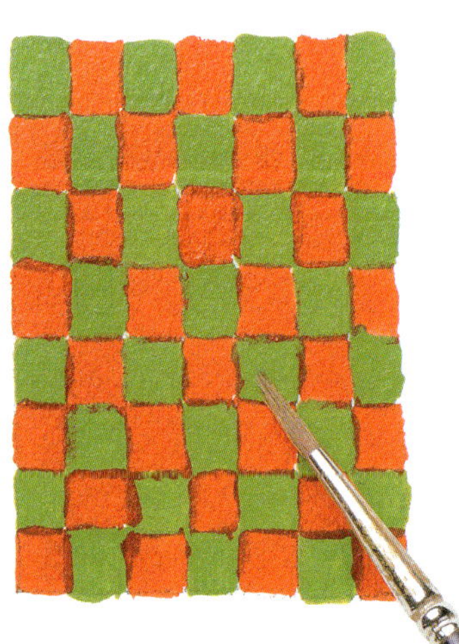

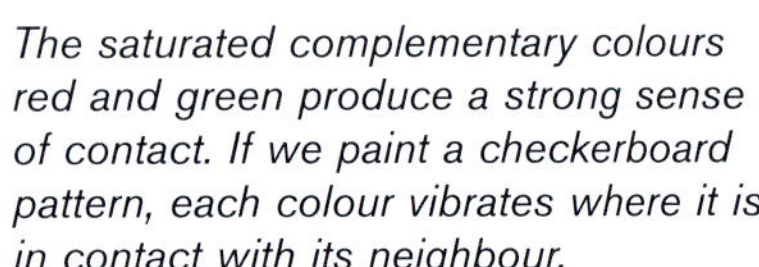

The saturated complementary colours red and green produce a strong sense of contact. If we paint a checkerboard pattern, each colour vibrates where it is in contact with its neighbour.

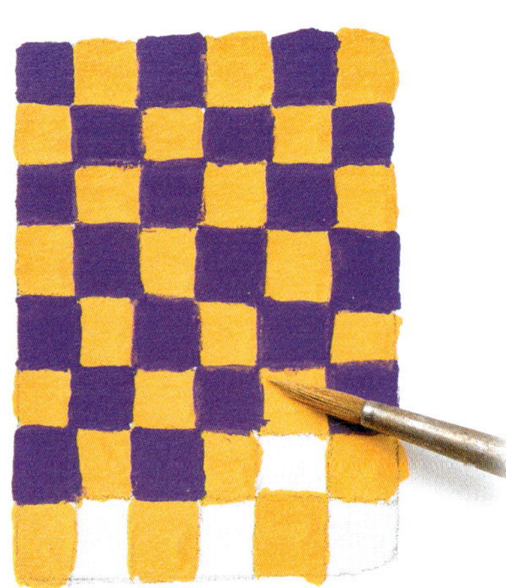

The same happens with yellow and violet. Here however the vibration is less because of the great difference in value between the two colours.

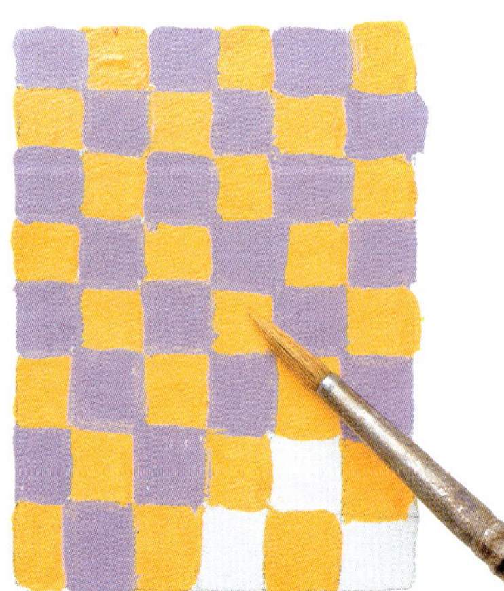

To recapture the vibration between the two complementary colours, both should be of a similar value.

If we observe the edges where the two complementary colours meet, we will see that they intensify each other. This optical effect causes the appearance of a thin imaginary line that separates them. This effect disappears when the colours are separated by wide white areas.

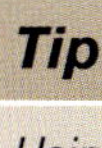

Tip

Using carefully selected backgrounds of different colours, the effect of simultaneous contrast can cause two physically different tones to seem the same.

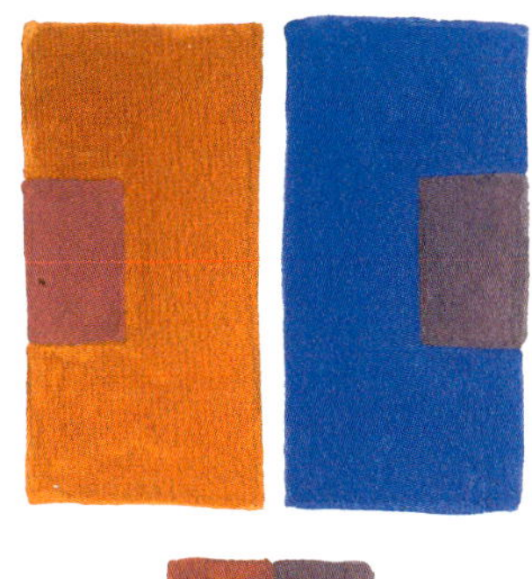

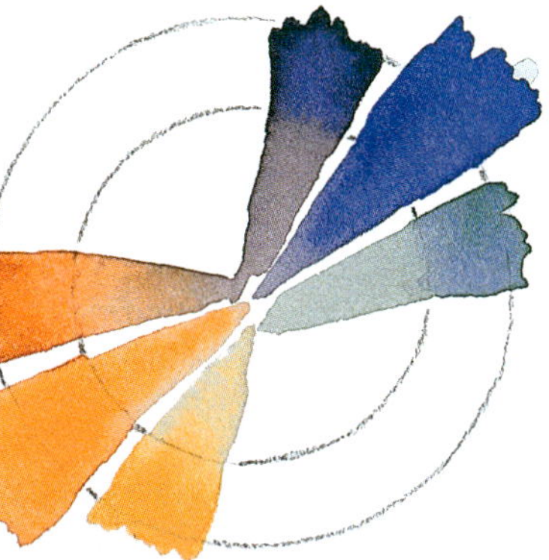

When using complementary colours, it is interesting to include split complementary schemes, which means using the colours adjacent to the complementary colours on the colour wheel.

Induced Complementary Colours

To understand the induction of complementary colours you can simply look at a grey circle surrounded by an intense orange, which gives the grey circle a bluish tint; red will make the grey seem greenish and yellow turns it slightly mauve.

Split Complementary Colours

It is more interesting to use the split complementary colours than the absolute ones, since they are more attractive. Using two adjacent tones on the colour wheel along with their respective complements is known as a split complementary colour scheme; for example, violet is the complement of yellow, while its split complements are blue violet and red violet.

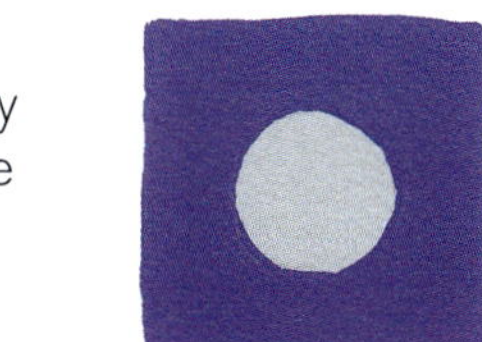

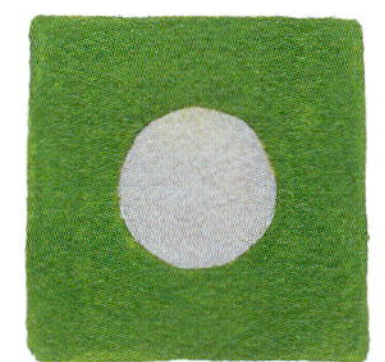

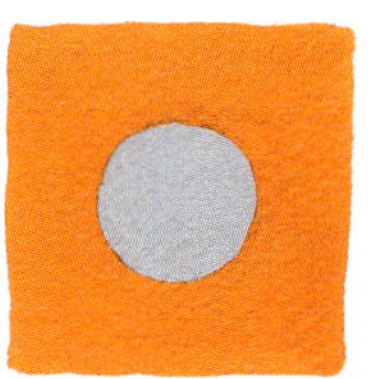

Saturated colours influence the visual effect of a neutral grey by inducing its complement. Therefore, an orange square causes the grey circle to look blue, the green makes it red, and the violet gives it a yellow tendency.

MAKING A COLOUR LIGHTER USING SIMULTANEOUS CONTRAST

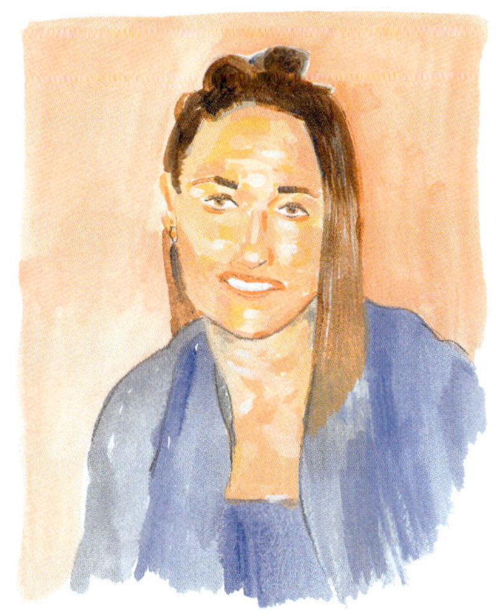

This model is painted with very light pink, ochre and blue colours. We are not satisfied with the tone of the face and we want to lighten it so it will stand out more.

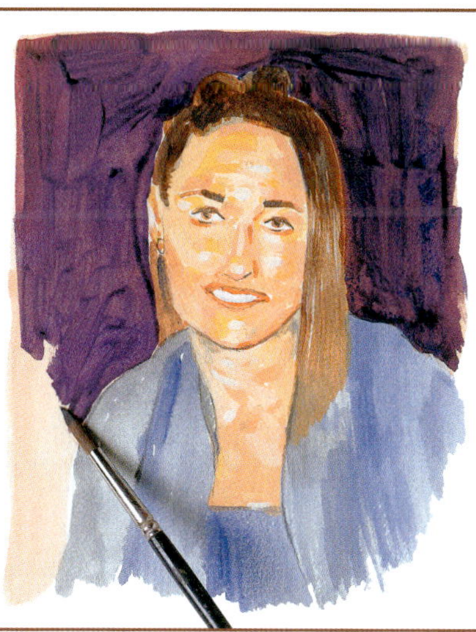

Instead of repainting the skin tones on the face with lighter colours, we will lighten them using simultaneous contrast. In other words, we will darken the adjacent colours.

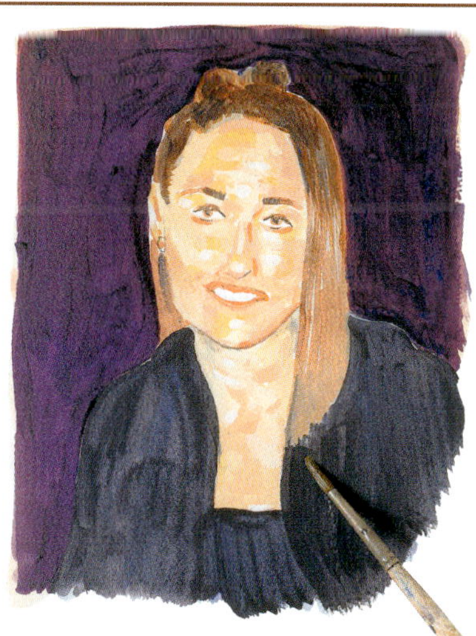

We cover the background with violet and paint the clothing with Payne's grey. The contrast between the lights and darks creates a greater sense of light on the face.

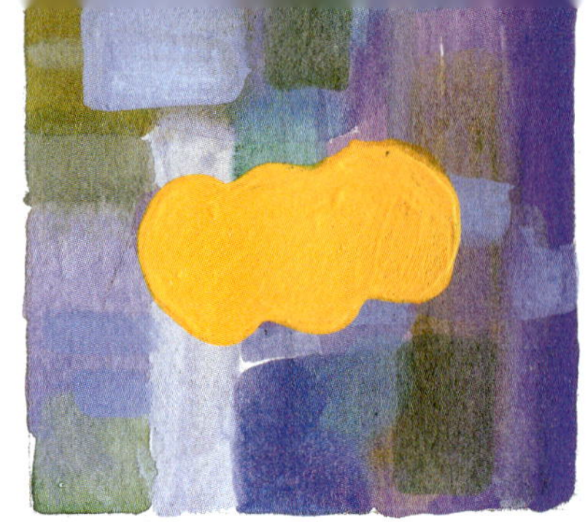

If we place a single area of warm colour on a background of cool colours, it will make the subject jump out and become the focal point.

COMPOSITION
Through Colour

Colour makes a considerable contribution to the composition of a painting. It creates visual structure through a more or less clear distribution of the contrasts of light and colour. The contrasts of colour ranges and colour saturation help create the focal point of the painting, the spatial limits and the relative abstract sensations of the space.

Emphasizing the Subject

The aim of many artists is to emphasize specific areas of a work to capture the attention of the viewer. One strategy consists of reducing the visual importance of everything around the subject so that it will stand out more through contrast; another is to paint the background using a cool range of colours while the main subject is done in bright, warm colours. You must be careful that the intense colour contrast is at the focal point of the painting; if equally intense and contrasting colours are used in several areas, it will result in a confused image.

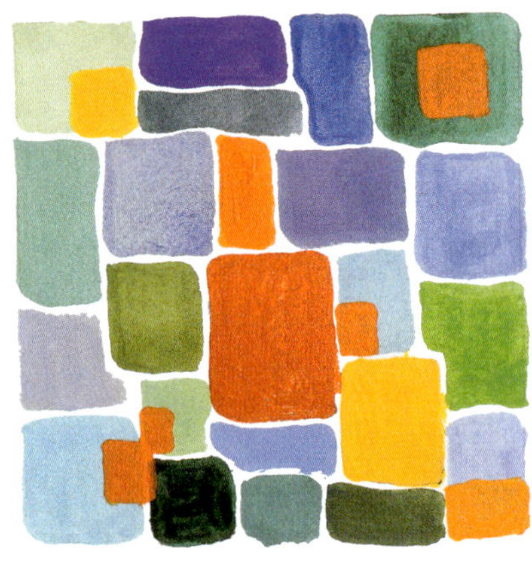

If we overuse this effect and paint several motifs using areas of warm colour over cool ones, the painting will seem unfocused and confusing to the viewer.

COLOUR CREATES ATMOSPHERE

The intensity of the colour, the contrasts and the distribution of the tones modify the perception of the space. An interior with strongly contrasting light creates a dramatic and theatrical atmosphere.

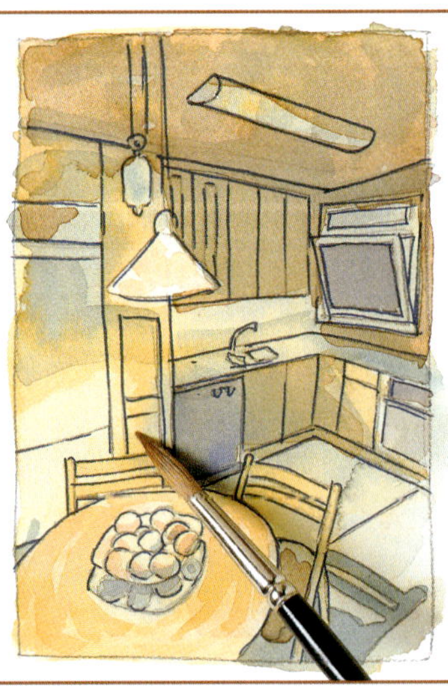

A range of neutral colours (ochres, browns and greys) harmonize well together, with no harsh contrasts. The result is a calm and peaceful feeling.

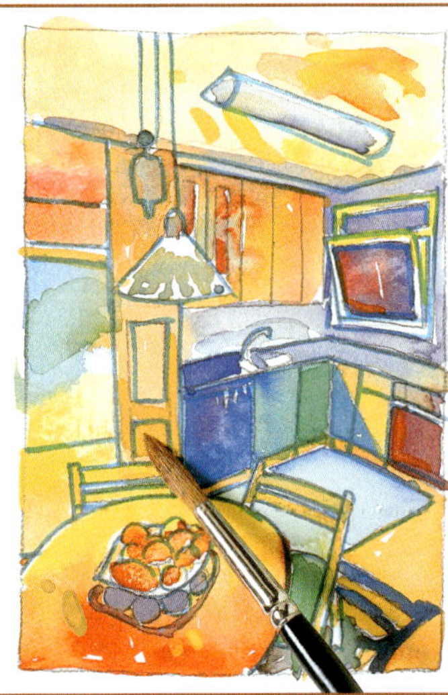

Saturated colour and strongly contrasting complements create a happy and lively interior. We lose the sensation of volume but we gain expressiveness.

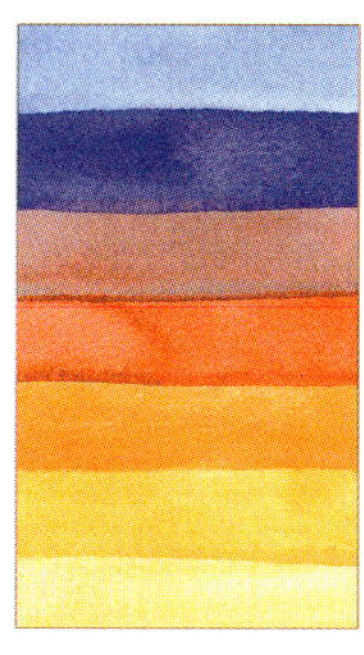

The colour yellow seems closer, as do the rest of the warm colours, while the green and blue tones seem farther away.

Tip

Gradations create a clear effect of depth, implying the passage of dark values to lighter ones, or vice versa. Colour gradations suggest the atmosphere of a landscape that fades into the distance, especially on foggy days.

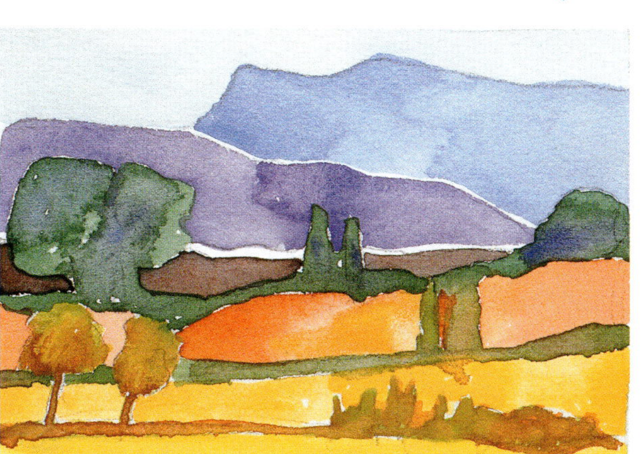

In this watercolour we apply the concept of advancing and receding colours using an analogous colour scheme.

Far and Near Colours

Contrasts in colour are greater in the areas that are closer to the viewer; they lose their saturation in the distance, and edges seem lighter, weaker and tinted by the blue atmosphere. The effect of distance can also be indicated by painting the closer objects with warm colours and the farthest ones with cool colours. The warm colours cause the objects to advance toward the viewer, while the cool colours recede.

Creating Atmosphere

In addition to helping organize the space, colour ranges and tone are essential for creating atmosphere. Spectacular contrasts of light and shadow with barely any middle tones create a theatrical atmosphere. A wide range of middle tones or a balanced tonal distribution usually creates a relaxed atmosphere; dark shades and saturated colours are more dynamic.

Creating Space

We can practise the optical effect of making small spaces seem larger using an interior. It is possible to make a ceiling seem lower if we paint it a colour that optically advances. In painting landscapes we can create spatial planes using warm colours that advance visually and cool colours that create a sense of receding.

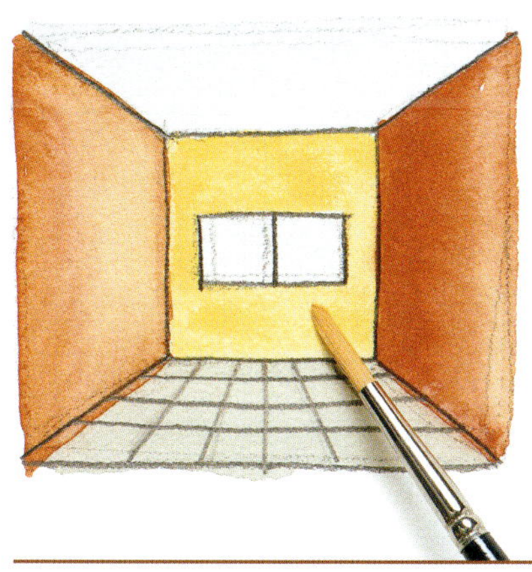

Let's test this concept. We will make a sketch of an interior and then paint its walls with warm colours, while the floor will be covered with a neutral colour wash.

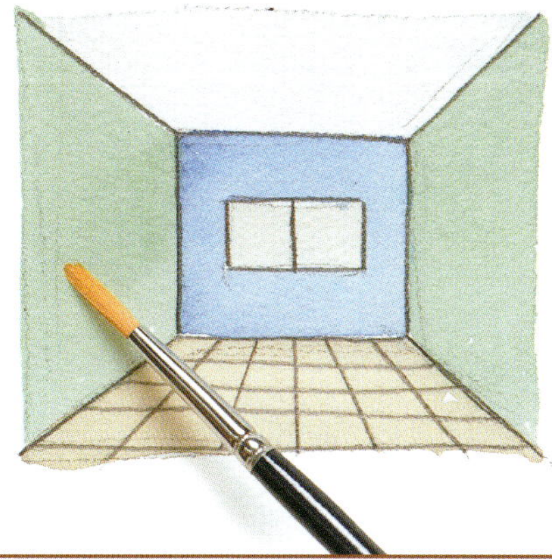

This time we will paint the walls with cool colours. Comparing the two paintings, we will see that the cool colours make the room feel larger and the warm ones make it smaller.

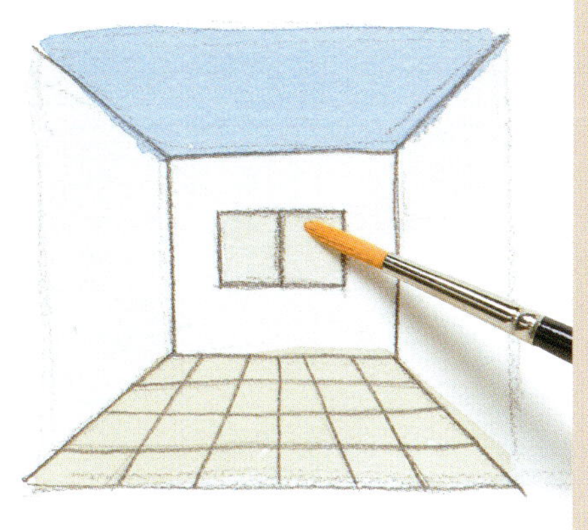

To make the room seem higher we paint the ceiling with cool colours.

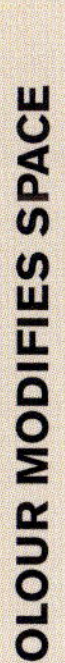

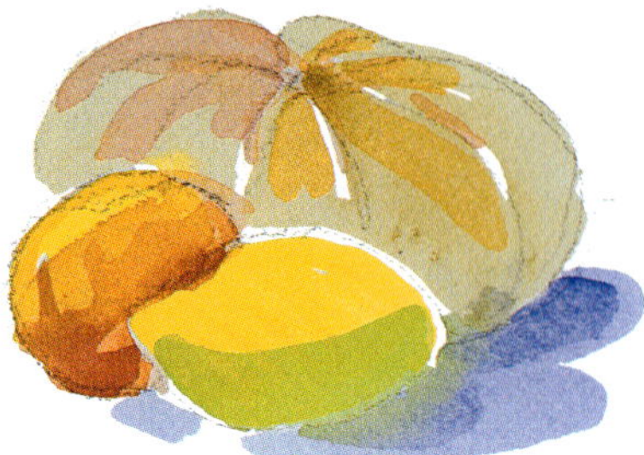

By superimposing several layers of clean and transparent colours, we achieve a brightly coloured subject.

MIXING
Colour on the Canvas

MIXING Colour on the Canvas

Learning to apply colours to the canvas or paper is the first step in creating a successful work of art. The artist must use his or her skills to create the illusion of a clear, bright light by applying warm and cool saturated colours to the canvas without previously mixing them on the palette.

Pointillism

The term "pointillism" is used to describe the technique of putting individual colours on the surface of the painting; in other words, juxtaposing small brushstrokes of saturated colour. The colours that are applied are not mixed very much, since the optical mixing takes place in the retina of the viewer. In this way, an area with dabs of paint in strokes of blue and yellow is perceived as green. Even real green strokes can be complemented with dabs of blue and yellow.

Optical Mixing

Optical mixing is based on the principle that a mass of individual colours are mixed "in the eye of the viewer" to form desired tones and shades. Optical mixing achieves better results than working with the palette, because the pigments do not mask each other and the brightness of the individual tones is not lost, even when they are seen as a mixture.

Pointillism creates a surface covered with short brushstrokes of saturated colour.

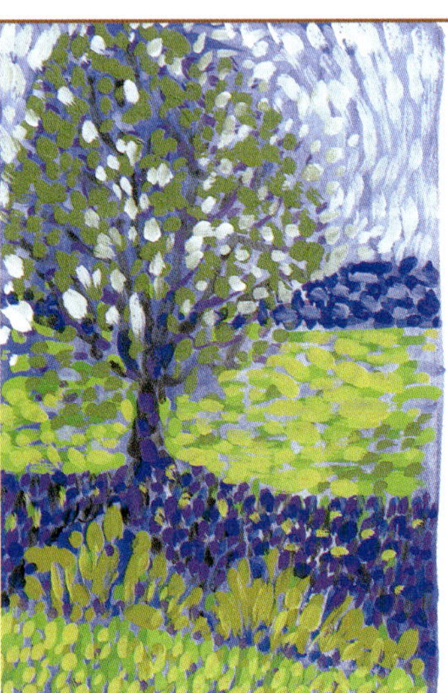

On a blue background, we cover different areas with small brushstrokes of green in the field and violet in the tree, the mountains and areas of shadow.

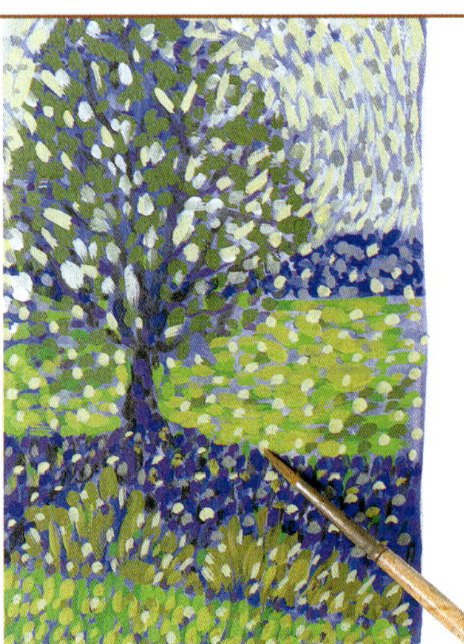

Over the previous base of colours, we lighten the sky with Naples yellow. This colour is distributed around the entire painting with spaced brushstrokes.

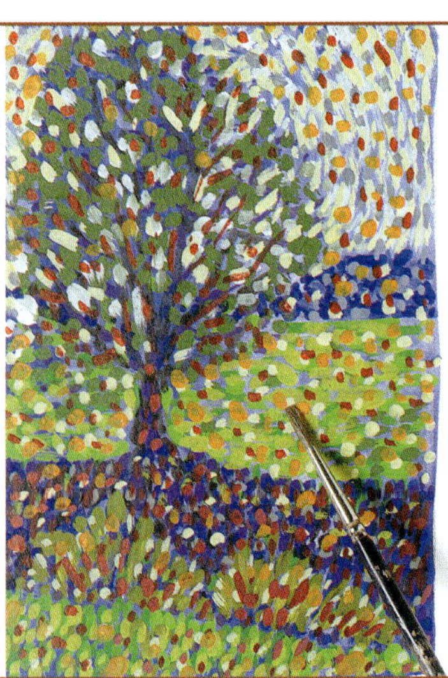

We finish it by applying red and orange brushstrokes. Although these colours do not appear in the real subject, they will add chromatic strength and help harmonize the subject if they are spaced well.

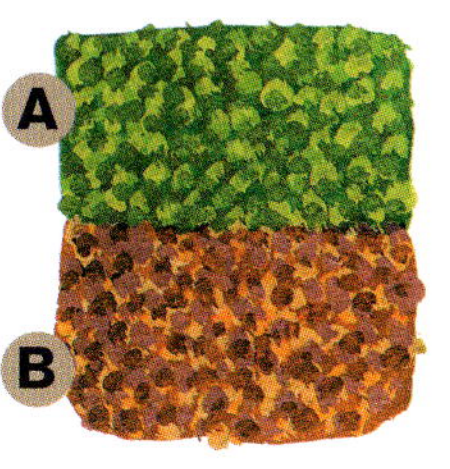

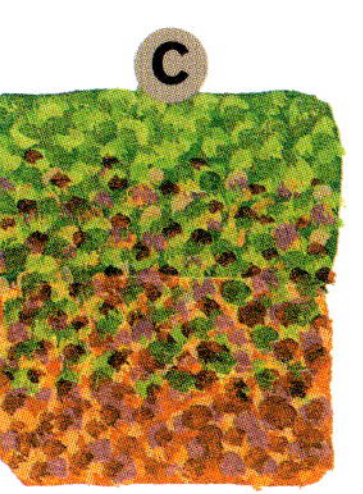

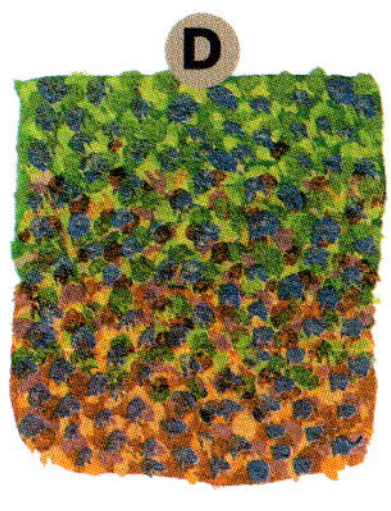

*Here we see three basic ways of working with pointillism. **(A)** The first consists of painting each area of colour with short brushstrokes from the same colour range. For example, a green area is covered with four different greens. **(B)** We can do the same with red. **(C)** The second method consists of blending the edges of the colour areas so that both are mixed in a middle area. **(D)** The final step is based on the previous gradation, to which we add new strokes of blue. Including a saturated contrasting colour in a uniform distribution helps to unify the painting.*

Tip

The smaller the dabs of colour, the more obvious the optical mixture. Keep in mind that this technique is based on colour harmony.

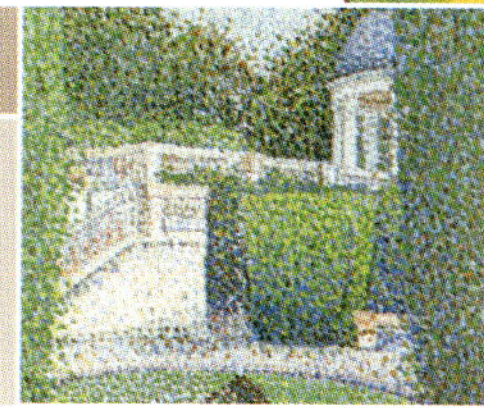

Superimposing Layers

Very rich mixtures of colour can be obtained using washes and diluted colours, with marvellous effects of depth and transparency. For this to be visually perfect, we must work with saturated colours. It can be a slow and laborious method, because of the amount of time it takes for each layer of colour to dry.

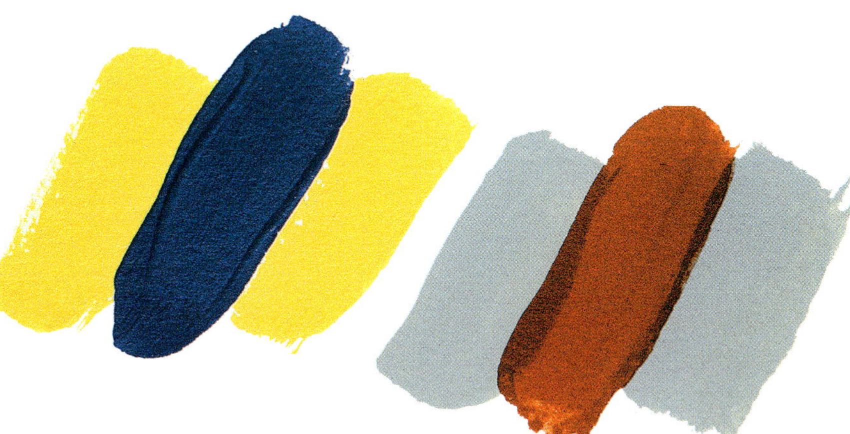

Colours Interact

Colours and tones should never be considered in isolation, but in the context of their relationship with those that surround them. Each new dab of colour that is added to a painting alters the relationship between the already existing colours: an intense red seems more intense between two light blue colours, and blue will seem darker if it is surrounded by light yellow brushstrokes.

When painting with short brushstrokes, keep in mind that bright colours increase in intensity next to neutral colours. Dark tones, on the other hand, seem more intense next to light ones.

It is possible to paint by overlaying diluted acrylic paint or watercolours. Here is a wash made with blue, green and yellow.

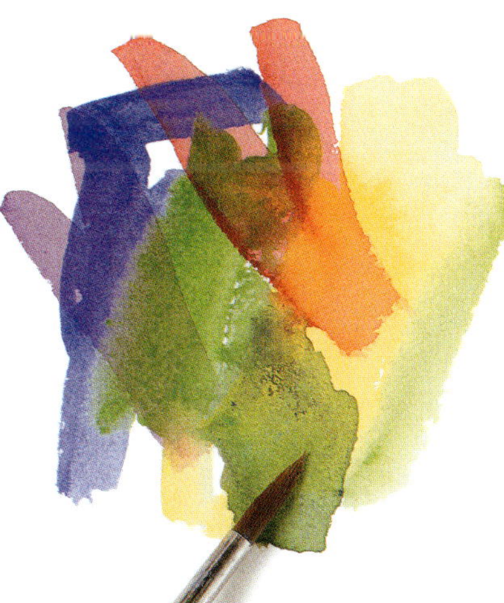

After the colour has dried, we overlay a new wash with various colours.

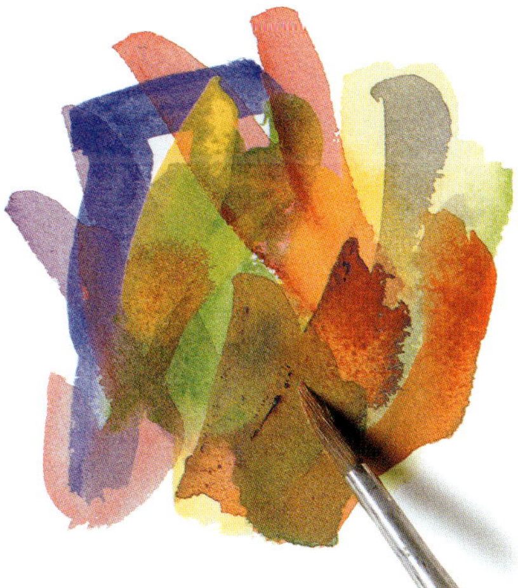

The colours are modified as they are superimposed. If we want the edges of the brushstrokes to be visible, we can allow each layer to dry before applying the next one.

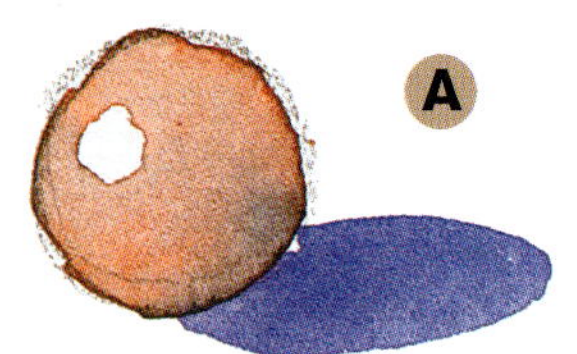

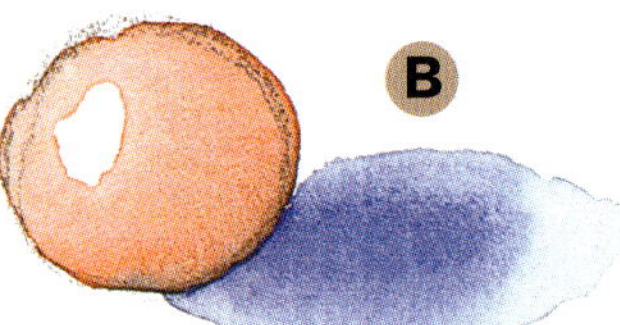

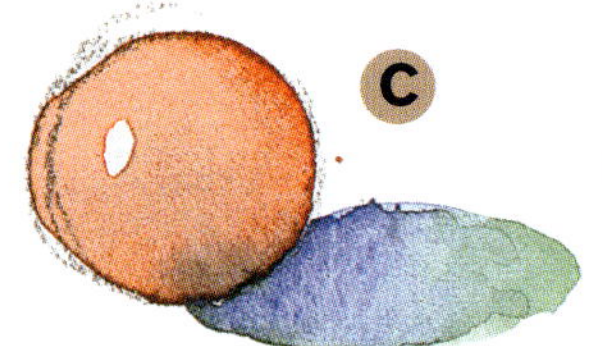

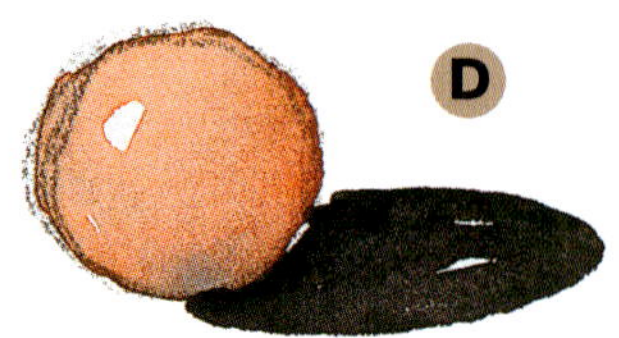

The Colour of SHADOWS

A shadow is an extension of the object in space, produced by light. It can be interpreted as a negative form; however, in works with strong colours it can capture the artist's attention to the point of becoming a determining element in the chromatic balance of the painting.

A. *To create a strong shadow we apply a uniform wash to dry paper. This will give us clear edges.*
B. *If we carry out the previous step on damp paper, the shadow will be blurry.*
C. *The colour of the shadow does not necessarily have to be uniform; two colours can even be mixed to make a gradation.*
D. *The darkest colour is an intense black, which gives the work a particularly striking graphic impact.*

Shadows with Colour

The shadow that a body projects on the ground during a sunny day is a dark mass that indicates a lack of light, but this does not mean that when you paint it, the lack of luminosity should translate into a lack of colour. Sometimes the effects of light and shadow cause the colour to become apparent; the contrast can be more effective if blue or green colours appear in the shadow to stimulate a contrasting colour range or to complement the sunny areas.

Corporeality of the Shadow

Tonal contrasts are usually stronger with projected shadows that have well-defined edges than with graduated shadows with soft edges. This gives the shadow a corporeality that it often does not have.

DARING SHADOWS

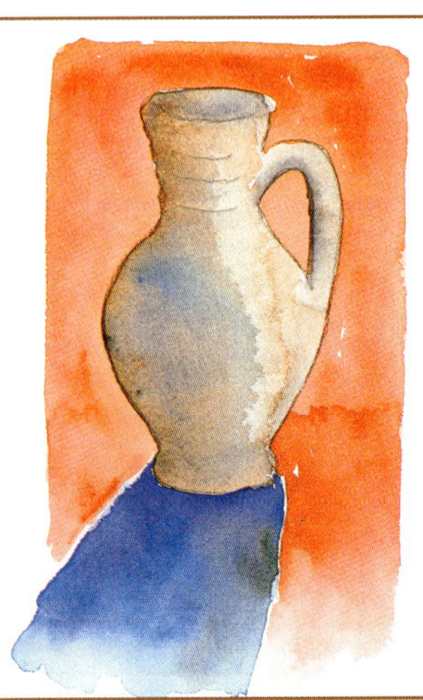

In colourist works we can paint the shadows with bright colours to create the greatest contrasts. Violet, blue and their derivatives are an excellent option.

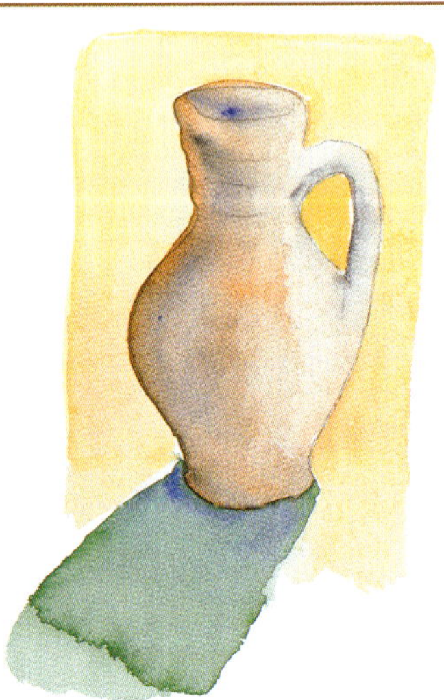

Green shadows are less common than blue ones, but they create a strong visual impact when the dominant colour in the painting is yellow or red.

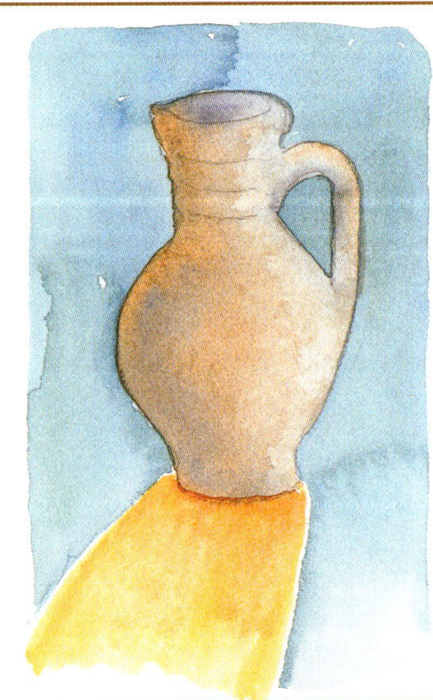

We can commit the error of painting the shadows orange or yellow. It is not a good idea to use warm colours for this, since they will seem like rays of light rather than shadows.

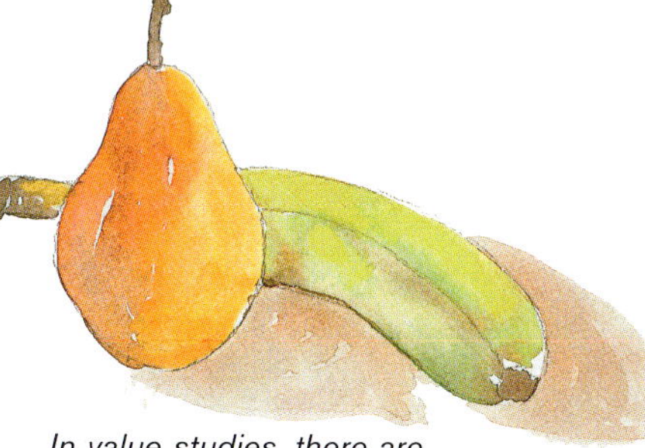

In value studies, there are barely any colours in the shadow. Neutral colours or grey work better.

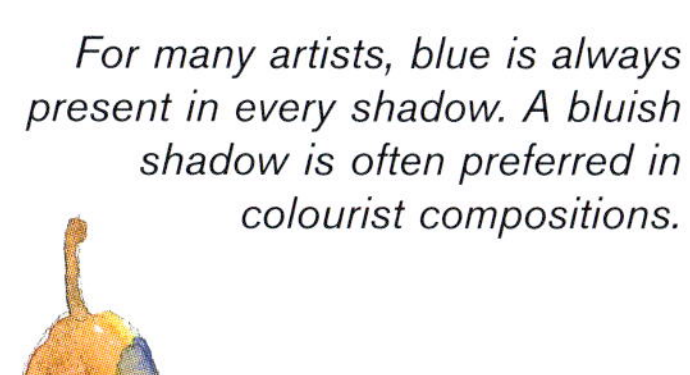

For many artists, blue is always present in every shadow. A bluish shadow is often preferred in colourist compositions.

Tip

Many artists begin their watercolours by placing the shadows with blue washes. This differentiates the illuminated areas from the shaded areas from the beginning.

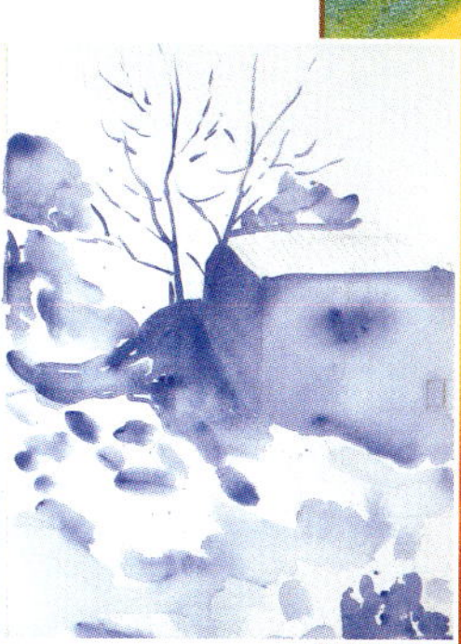

Different Shading: Value Study

There are three different ways to paint a shadow. The most common is to paint it using a colour from the same range, only in a darker tone. The Renaissance and Baroque artists used chiaroscuro contrasts to intensify the shaded areas; the value study approach of resolving the colour of the shadows is therefore reminiscent of those works.

Blue Shadows

At the height of the Impressionist movement, shadows adopted a blue or violet colour. This change of attitude toward colour was based on the belief that if the maximum incidence of light is represented by the colour yellow, the darkness should not be black, but the opposite colour on the colour wheel, violet.

Shadows with Complementary Colours

Another option is to always paint the shadow using the complementary colours of the lighted areas. For example, an intense blue in the shadow of an orange ceramic pitcher or a green shadow complementing the red of an apple. The Fauvist painters frequently used this principle of complements to create works that were beautiful symphonies of light and colour.

The shadow projected by the red objects can be painted with their complement, green.

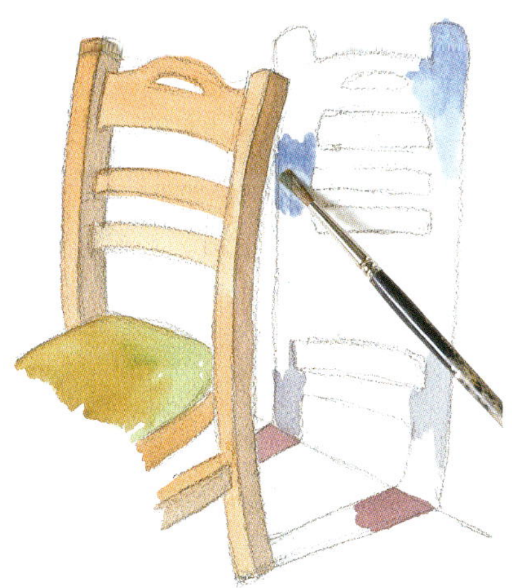

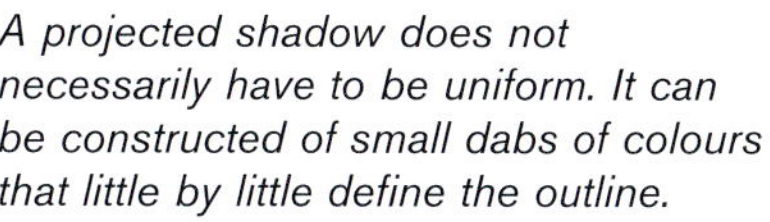

A projected shadow does not necessarily have to be uniform. It can be constructed of small dabs of colours that little by little define the outline.

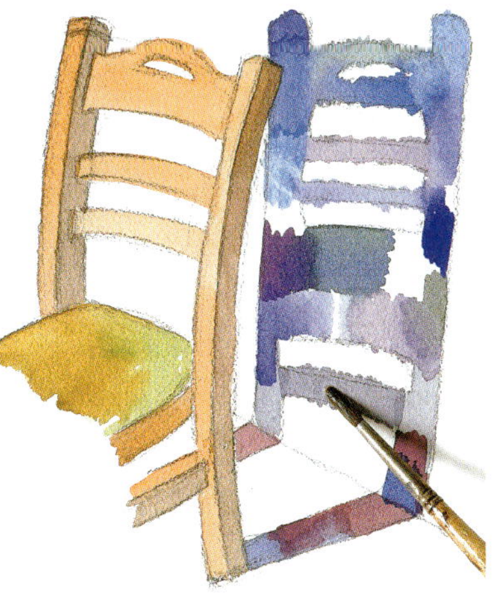

Violet, grey-blues and blue-greens are added. Some of the colours run together to form gradations; others stand alone.

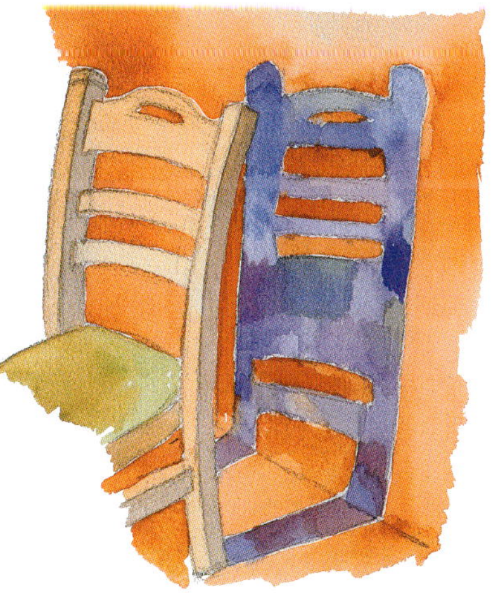

All that remains is to complete the outline of the shadow with the last additions of blue. For greater contrast, we cover the background with cadmium red.

CHROMATIC SCHEMES

When the chromatic effects of a subject are complex and varied, two different options are available. We can deal with them in a very thorough manner or approach the subject in a more selective way, revising the intensity of the shades and tones to organize the similarities and oppositions in a more deliberate manner. Here we analyze four basic methods for developing chromatic schemes that make the subject easier to understand.

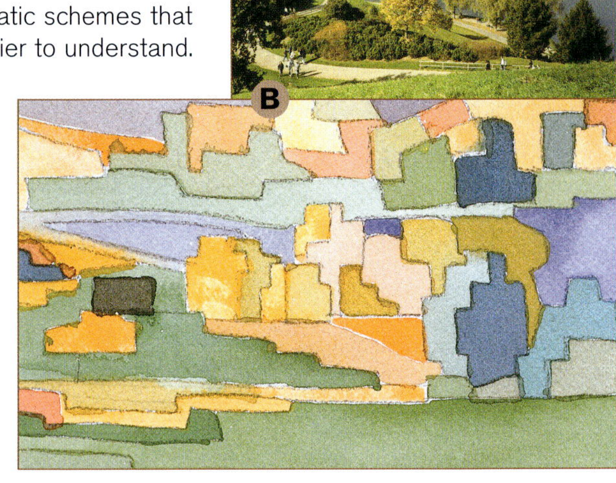

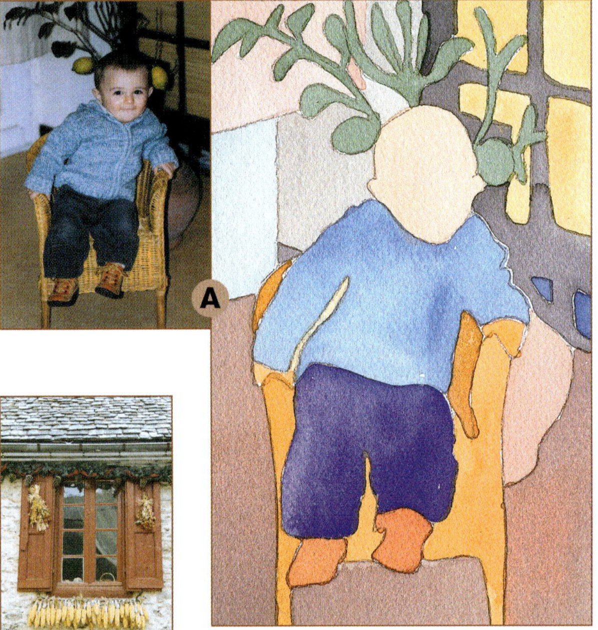

Chromatic Mass (A)
One of the fundamental chromatic schemes helps simplify and unify the different areas of colour in the painting. After they are simplified, they are treated as flat washes.

Working in Blocks (B)
A landscape with a great variety of tones and values can be simplified with a drawing of geometric shapes, with blocks that enclose each different area of colour. Then each colour is painted inside its corresponding shape.

Inventing Colours (D)
Faced with a subject with few chromatic variations, it becomes necessary to invent colours where they do not exist. This model is dominated by greys, but the resulting chromatic scheme is rich in colours and contrasts that make the subject more attractive.

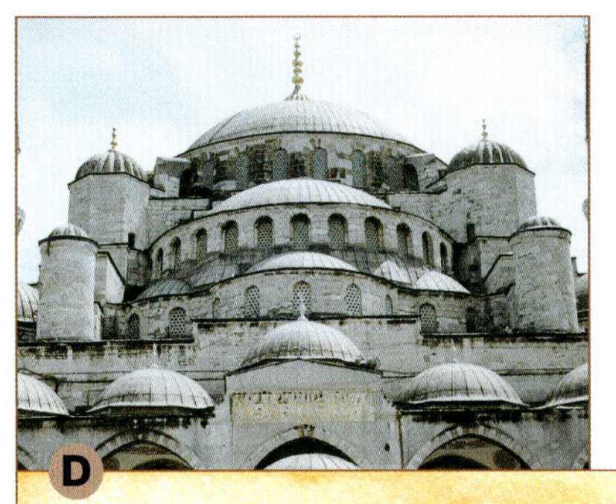

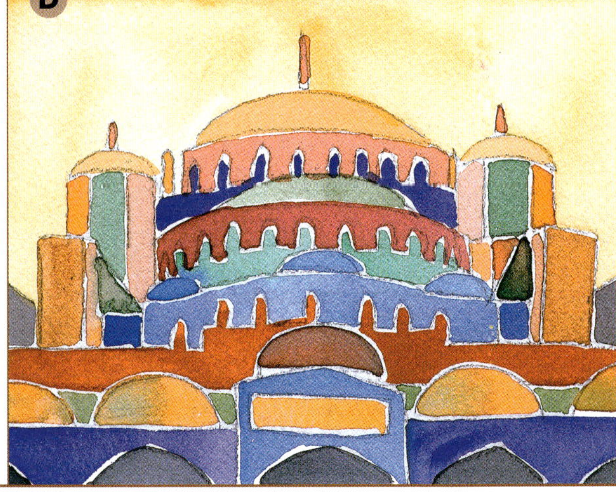

Grid Scheme (C)
This is a very complex method that permits a more thorough study of the subject. A grid is drawn on a photograph of the subject and on the sheet of paper. Then each square is painted in the dominant colour of the corresponding square in the photograph. This will give us a fragmented image with valuable chromatic information about the model.

COLOUR TRANSMITS *and* CREATES SPACE

The correct choice of one or another colour in a subject is essential for transmitting a specific feeling to the viewer. Striking contrasts, as well as the use of warm and saturated colours, are the main ways of creating visual excitement. But it is not enough to arbitrarily place the colours on the surface of the painting – we should maintain an order, since the effect of depth in the work depends on this.

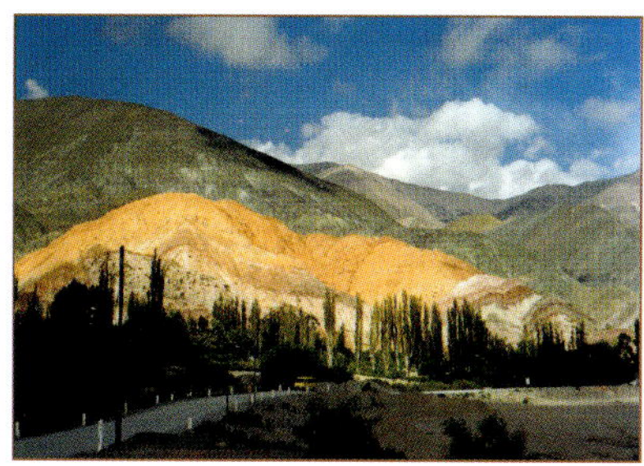

The starting point for our analysis is this mountain landscape with clearly differentiated grounds.

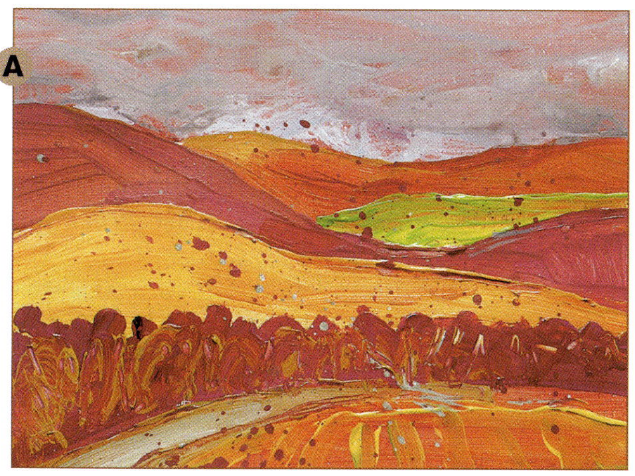

***A.** Saturated red, yellow, orange and magenta colours fill this composition. The selection of this range of colours affects the perception of the landscape, which seems to smoulder under a burning sun.*

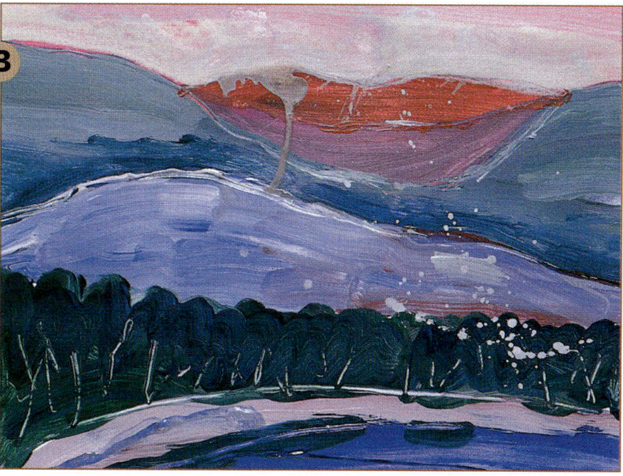

***B.** Using an opposite approach, the same landscape is constructed with bands of cool colours. There is much less excitement here, and the light that illuminates the landscape seems more subdued. It transmits a greater feeling of tranquillity and a colder environment, typical of a winter scene.*

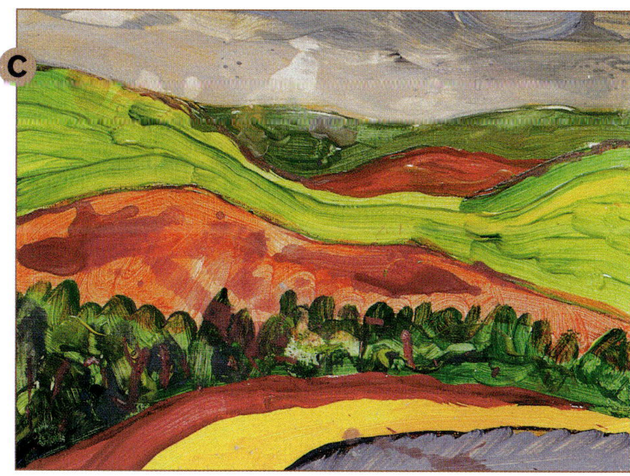

***C.** In this new example, we recapture the feeling of excitement achieved through the extreme contrasts between the bands of warm and cool saturated colours. However, the space is quite ambiguous and incoherent. It is not able to communicate the effect of depth that is so evident in the two previous cases, since it seems that the distant mountains advance more than the foreground.*

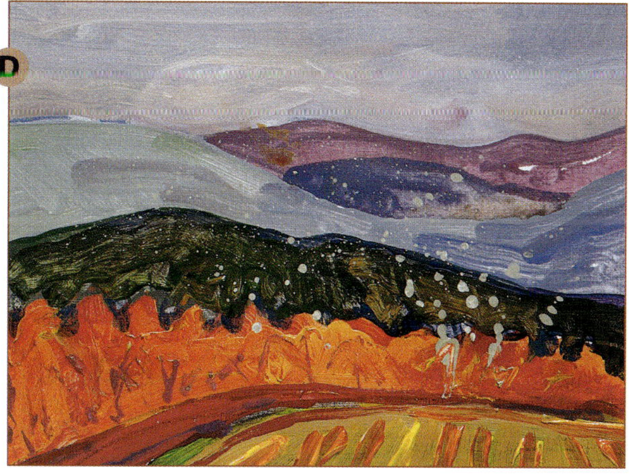

***D.** If we keep in mind that warm colours advance and cool ones recede, this should suggest the correct way to arrange the colours in a colourist landscape. The foreground is painted with saturated oranges and reds that move toward the viewer, and a sort of green colour is in the middle ground. Cool colours are dominant in the far mountains, reinforcing the effect of depth.*

Colour HARMONIES

The close relationship between tones of the same family creates a natural harmony in which colour unifies the forms and structures of the composition. This does not exclude the possibility of adding counter-points of another colour, as long as it does not create too much contrast.

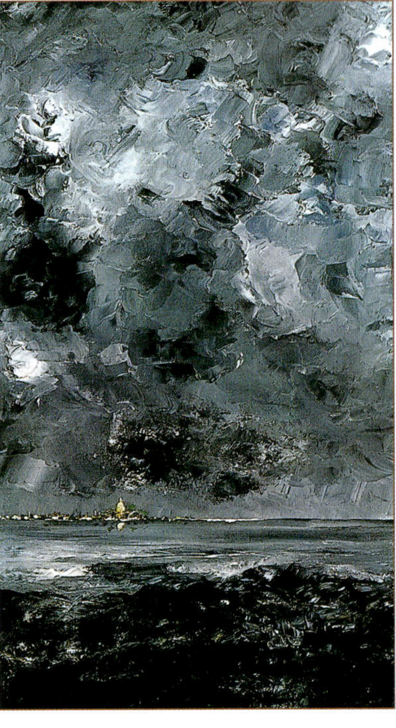

The purest and strongest monochromatic studies are those that use only black and white.

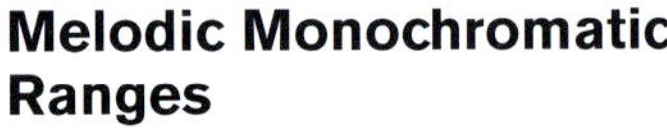

Melodic Monochromatic Ranges

Using a single colour as a base, the entire image is created through changes in value and tone. If the value is changed using only white and black or the complement, it is a monochromatic study. If the tone is also changed, it is called a simple melodic range or dominant tone range. In this case, we mix the base colour with others to shade it while maintaining the character of the dominant tone. Very suggestive monochromatic harmonies can be achieved with a few changes of tone and value.

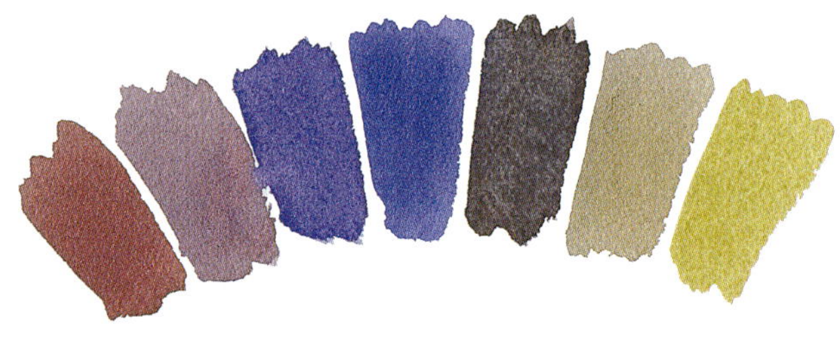

The harmonic ranges of a single colour are created by mixing it with other colours that are adjacent to it on the colour wheel.

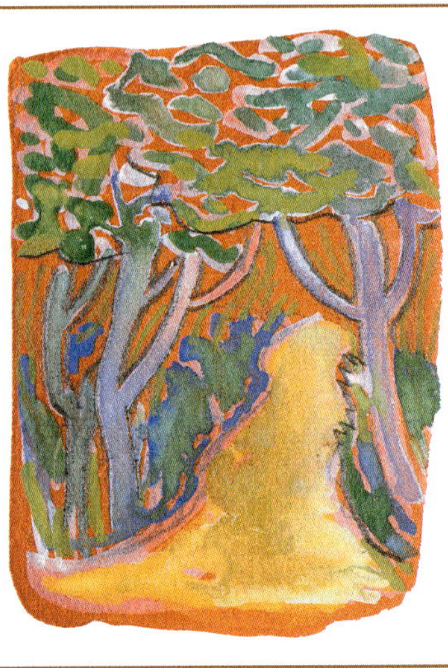

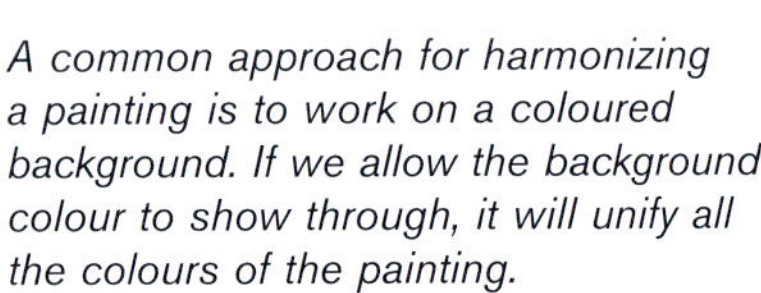

A common approach for harmonizing a painting is to work on a coloured background. If we allow the background colour to show through, it will unify all the colours of the painting.

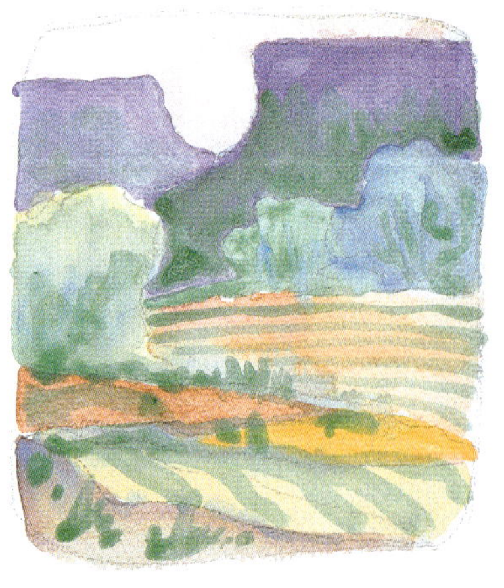

Repeating the same colour in different areas of the painting can also produce a unifying effect. The repetition of the green tones in the different grounds of the landscape harmonizes the painting.

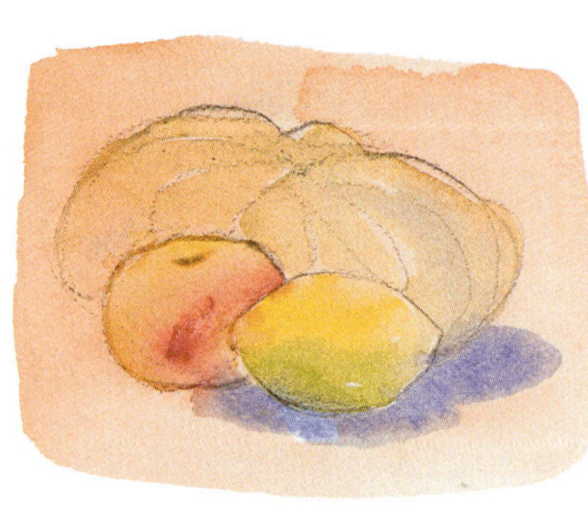

If we want the colours of a subject to harmonize with each other, we can choose to cover the entire picture with a glaze or wash of colour.

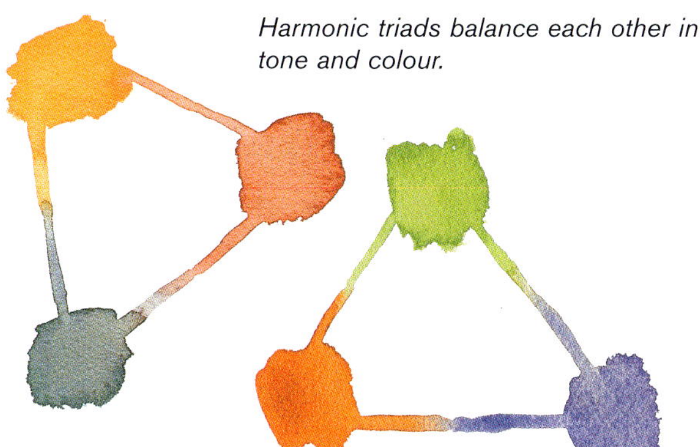
Harmonic triads balance each other in tone and colour.

Tip

Neutral colours are essential for harmony in a painting. These are greys with tendencies towards a colour. They are created by mixing complementary colours with each other.

The Dominant Role

Just like in landscapes, all subjects have a dominant colour. They can also be organized in a way that colour connections are created. It can be a challenge to our ability as colourists to evaluate the similarities of the colours instead of discovering their differences, which is the more common approach.

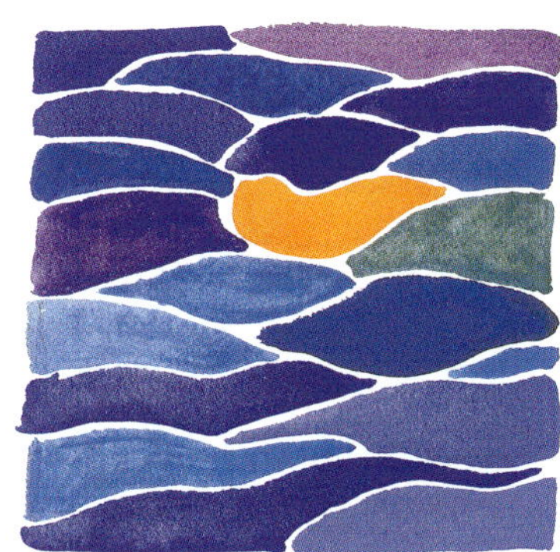
This scheme exemplifies the use of a complementary accent. An orange accent breaks the monotony of the blues and adds greater interest to the picture.

Harmonic Triads

This is a method of creating harmony in a painting by combining three colours that are equidistant on the colour wheel. The three colours form an equilateral triangle on the colour wheel, and although none is the complement of another (which eliminates tension), the three colours compensate for this in their luminosity and boldness.

Using a Background Colour

A background with a strong colour behind the subject can create a very interesting effect, and sometimes it greatly increases the visual impact of the subject. If we allow this background to be visible, showing through in different areas of the picture, it will notably unify the colours.

Harmony and Counterpoint

While a range of similar colours can create harmony, sometimes some contrast must be introduced to enrich the effect of the painting – an accent of colour to attract the viewer's attention, or a counterpoint. The chromatic difference can be tonal, a light or bright colour or it can be a contrast between complements or an opposition of warm and cool colours.

SKETCH WITH HARMONIC TRIADS

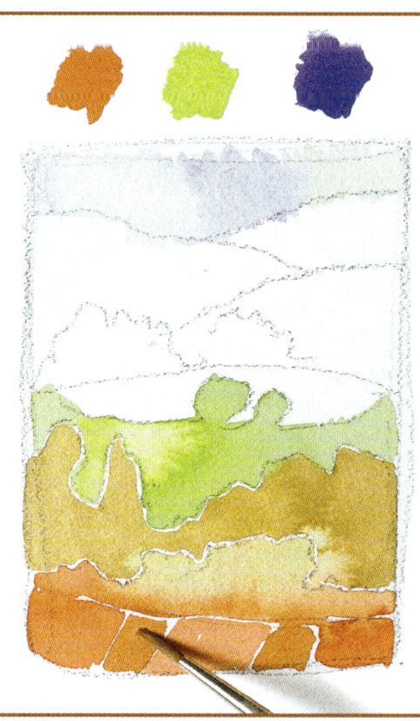
Here we paint a landscape with a triad of harmonic colours. The foreground is painted red. The middle ground is painted with a mixture of red and green, and green is painted behind that.

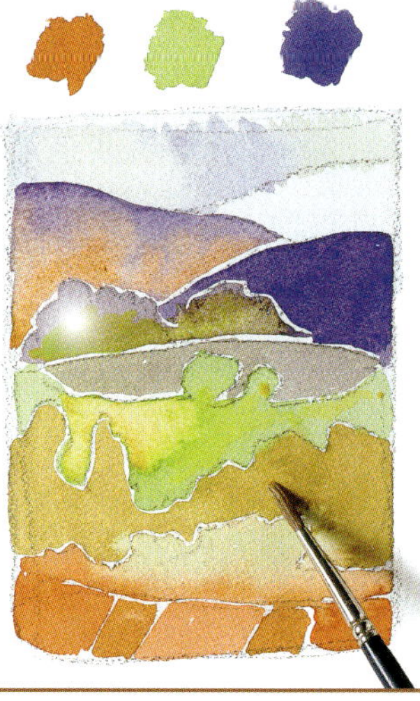
Now we add blue to the most distant planes: the outlines of the mountains. A touch of green and red are added to the washes to help tie them to the foreground.

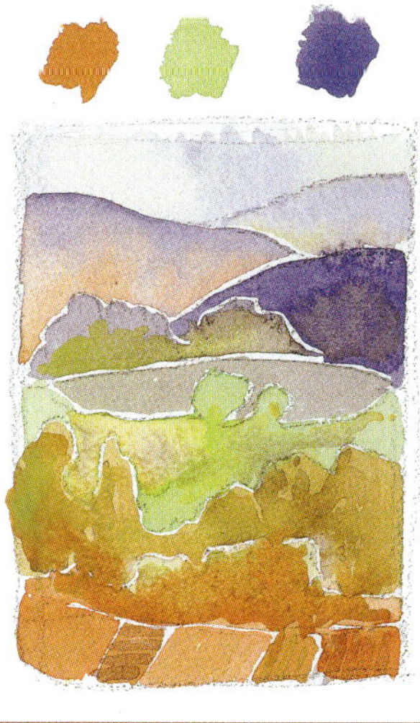
We then paint the farthest mountains and darken the lower washes. The combination of three harmonious colours results in a work with no chromatic dissonance.

LANDSCAPE *with* HIGH KEY COLOURS

SHEET

PRACTICE

In a landscape, the excessive presence of green can be a pitfall when it comes to incorporating chromatic variations that transmit light and energy. This problem can be resolved by mixing various tones of green with high key colours – pure tones like yellow, orange and blue – and combining them with existing greens to make them work.

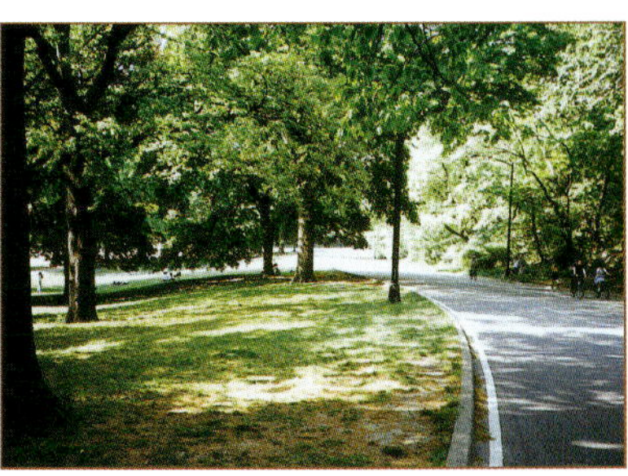

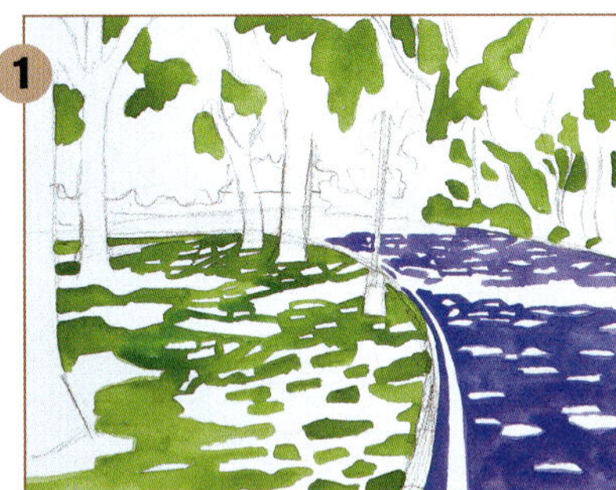

1. *We begin by making a pencil sketch. Our first goal is to cover the areas where the vegetation seems more homogeneous with a green layer. Then we paint the asphalt road with ultramarine blue.*

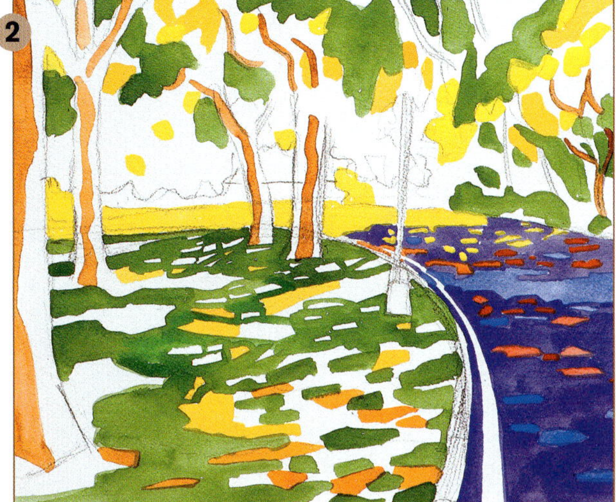

2. *The most luminous areas of foliage are painted with cadmium yellow, the lightest parts of the ground with yellow, the medium areas in orange and the light areas of asphalt in red and cyan blue.*

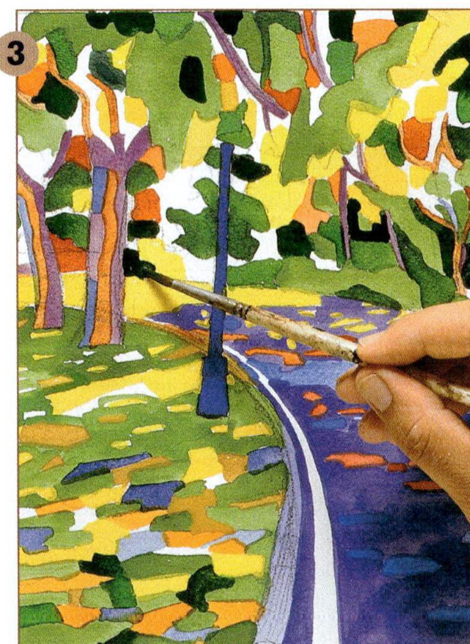

3. *The brushstrokes become smaller but with brighter colours. We try to be creative with the greens that we use, mixing them with blues, purples, reds and warm browns: ultramarine blue, Prussian blue, dark violet, carmine, red and burnt sienna.*

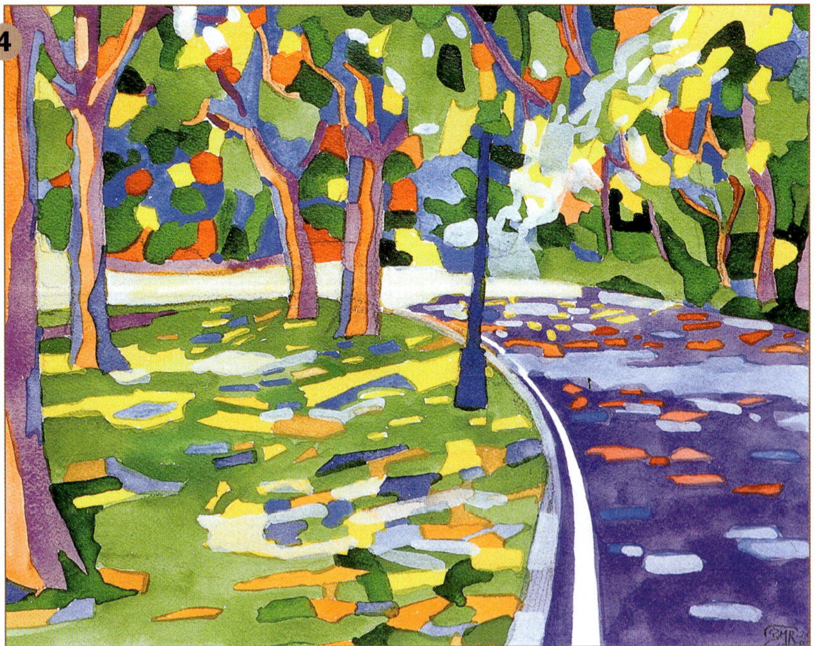

4. *Reds and blues now suggest the foliage in the trees, while yellows, ochres, blues and oranges indicate the leaves on the ground. To unify the brightest parts of the picture, we paint a layer of white gouache over the yellow in the background and the blue on the asphalt.*

Still Life with CONTRASTING COMPLEMENTS

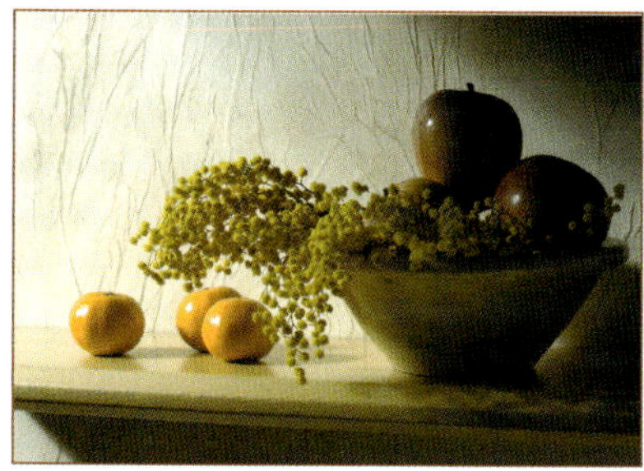

Red and green are probably the two complementary colours that contrast most strongly. Their medium tones create particularly attractive contrasts. In the following exercise, a still life, the combinations are painted with watercolour.

If we first make a small tonal scale by mixing the two colours in different proportions, we will see the richness of the intermediate tones.

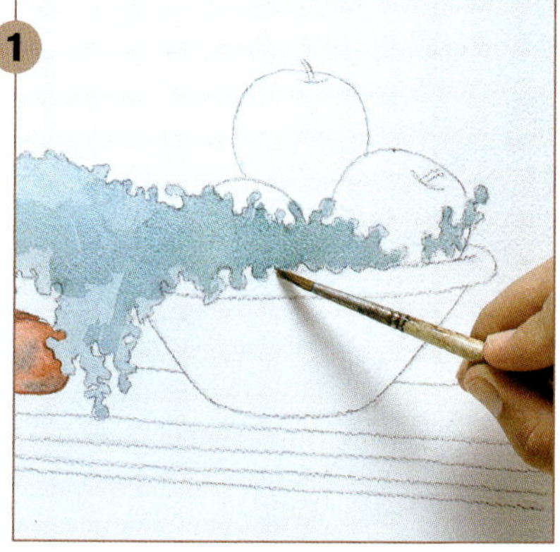

***1.** In the first phase, we paint the tangerines and the flowers using a limited range of tones: the mimosa with two tones of green and the three tangerines with red (to which we will apply a spot of green on the wet wash).*

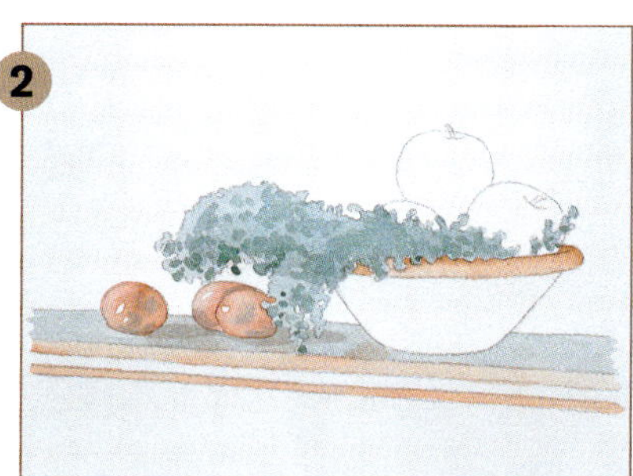

***2.** The shelf is painted with a medium grey, made by mixing equal parts of red and green. The shadows of the tangerines are painted over this with a reddish wash. The edges of the shelf and the bowl are then painted with a red wash.*

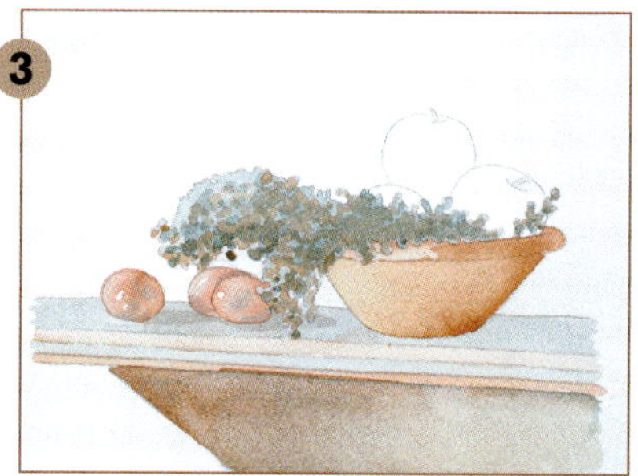

***3.** We then mix red with a little green and paint the shadow that the shelf projects on the wall. The body of the bowl is then painted with a graduated, light red wash.*

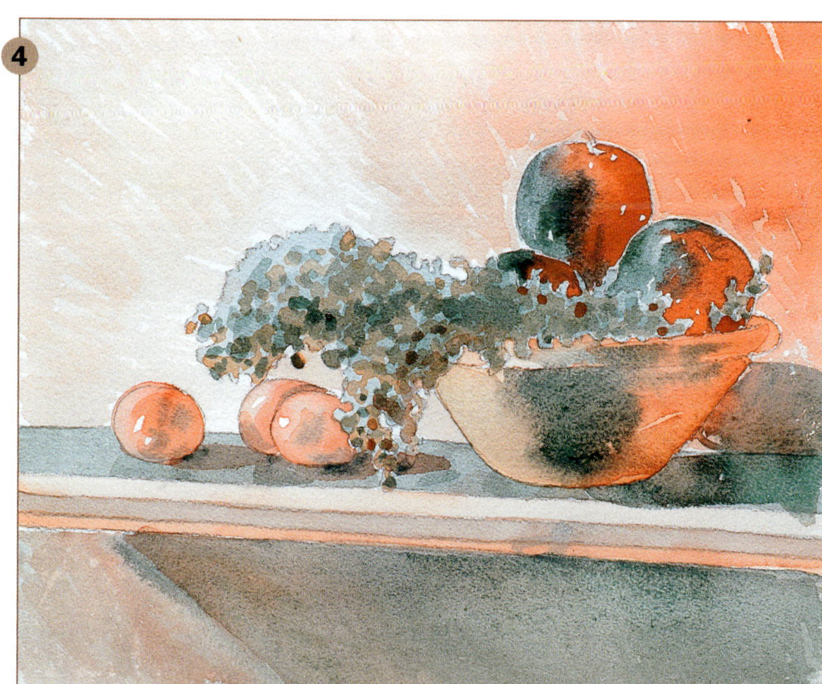

***4.** Now we paint the apples. We apply a dark wash to each side, one red and the other green, and blend them in the middle. New green washes are extended to the shadows of the bowl. To finish, we modify the tones and heighten some of the contrasts.*

PRACTICAL

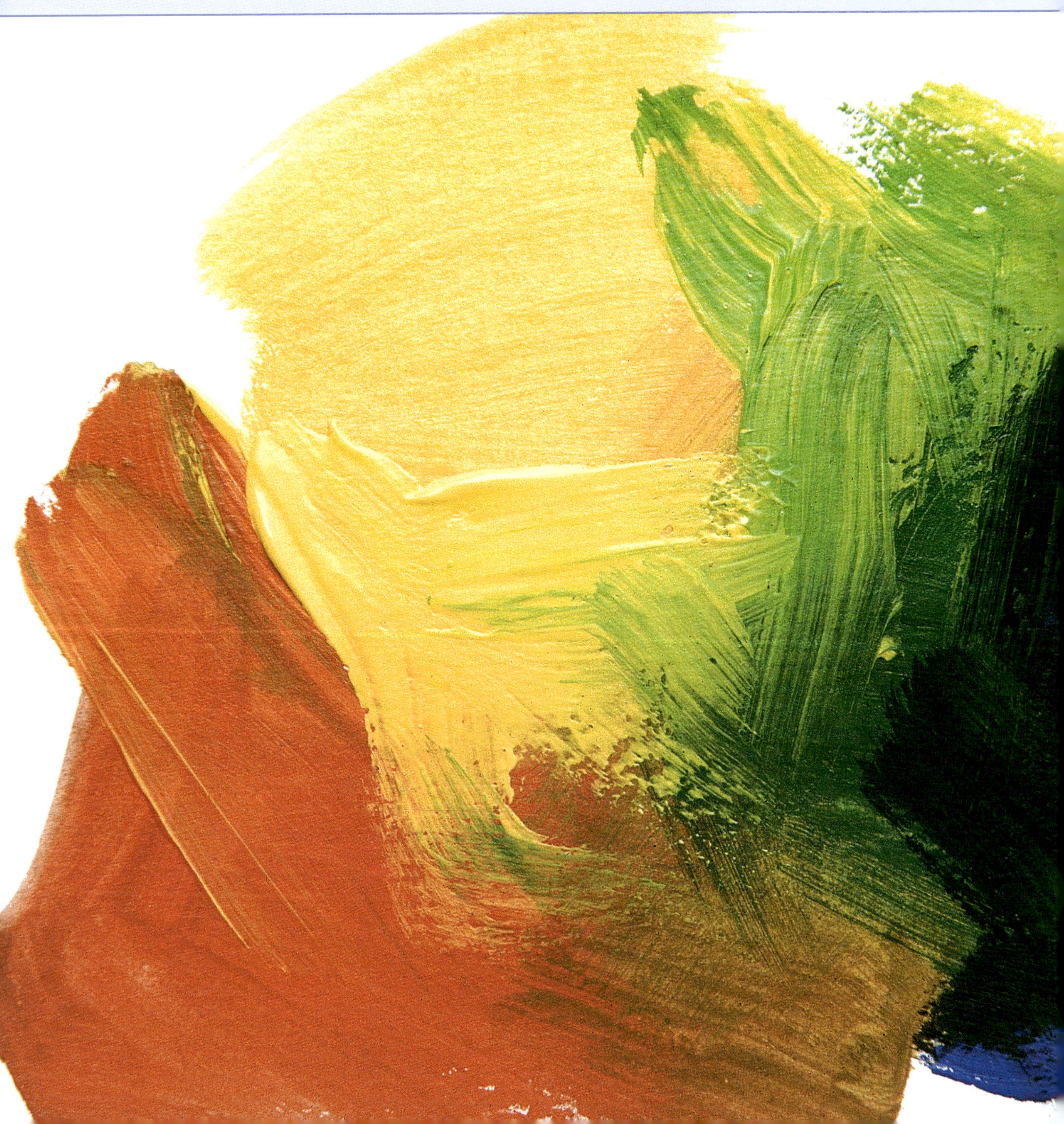

PRACTICAL EXERCISES

In this section, we develop the basic techniques for applying colour and explain the approaches required for transforming the actual subject into a colourful, expressive and creative work of art. If you work through the exercises, it will be possible to learn and improve quickly by following the process and the very simple advice. Each exercise introduces a different colour treatment, and suggests specific techniques and solutions for each case. Through these studies, you will find your own personal style, or you will discover which style to use according to what you wish to express.

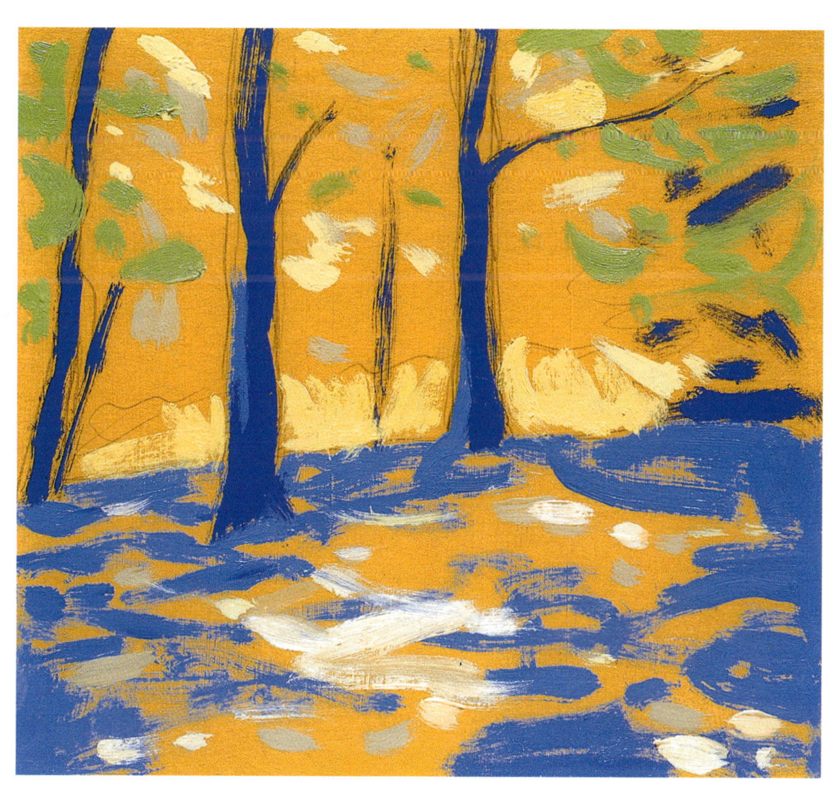

WARM *Colour Ranges*

STILL LIFE *with* *Warm Colour* RANGES

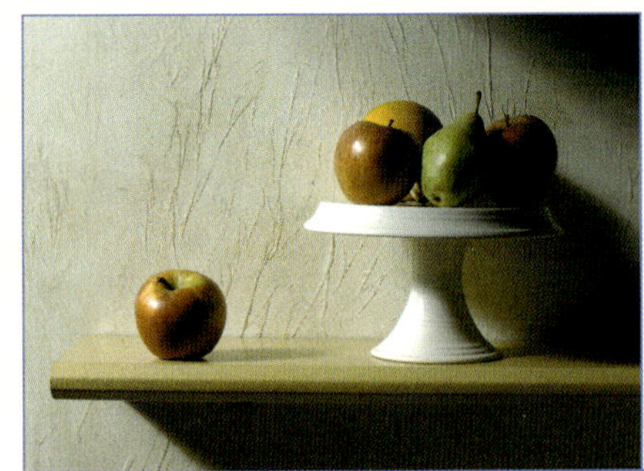

It can be quite practical to paint using a previously determined colour range. This is a good way to learn to control colour.

This exercise with gouache interprets a simple still life with a harmonious range of warm colours; this means translating the actual colours of the subject into others within the colour range. No cold colours are used in the mixture, so the red and orange tones clearly become dominant.

1

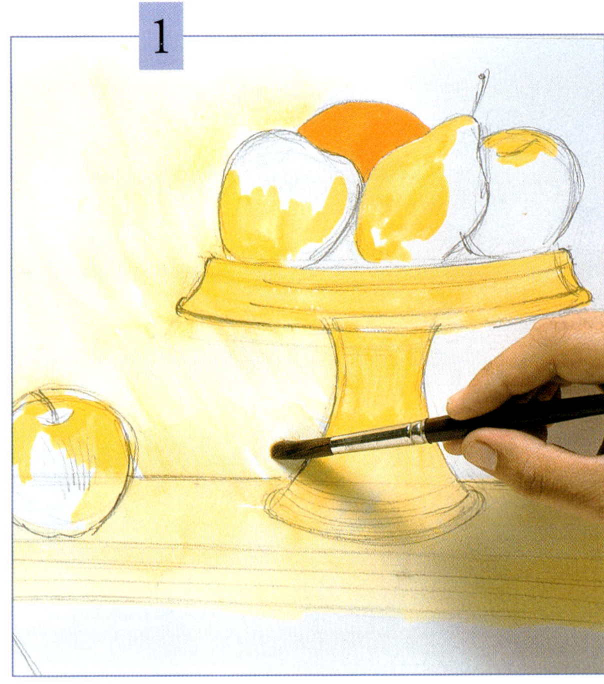

We sketch the model. The first strokes of colour are yellow. A very transparent yellow is used to cover the background. The fruit and the fruit stand are painted with orange and a more saturated version of the same yellow.

2

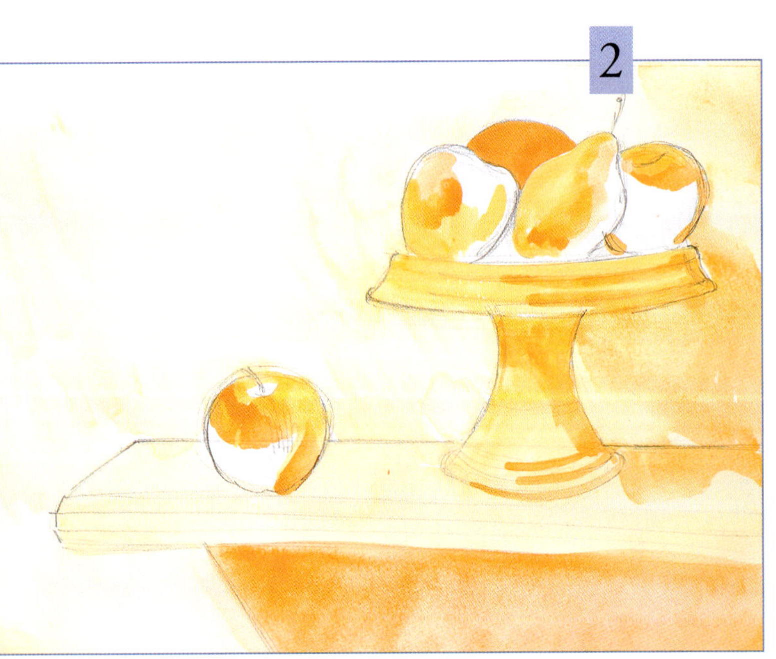

A little red is added to the yellow on the palette and mixed to make orange. We use it to add new transparent brushstrokes on the fruit and we indicate the shadows projected by the wood shelf and the fruit stand.

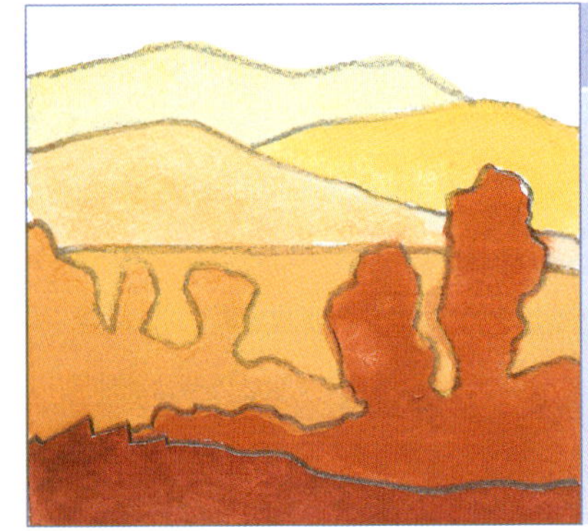

Tip

It is common to use the warm colours to communicate the heat of a summer landscape.

3

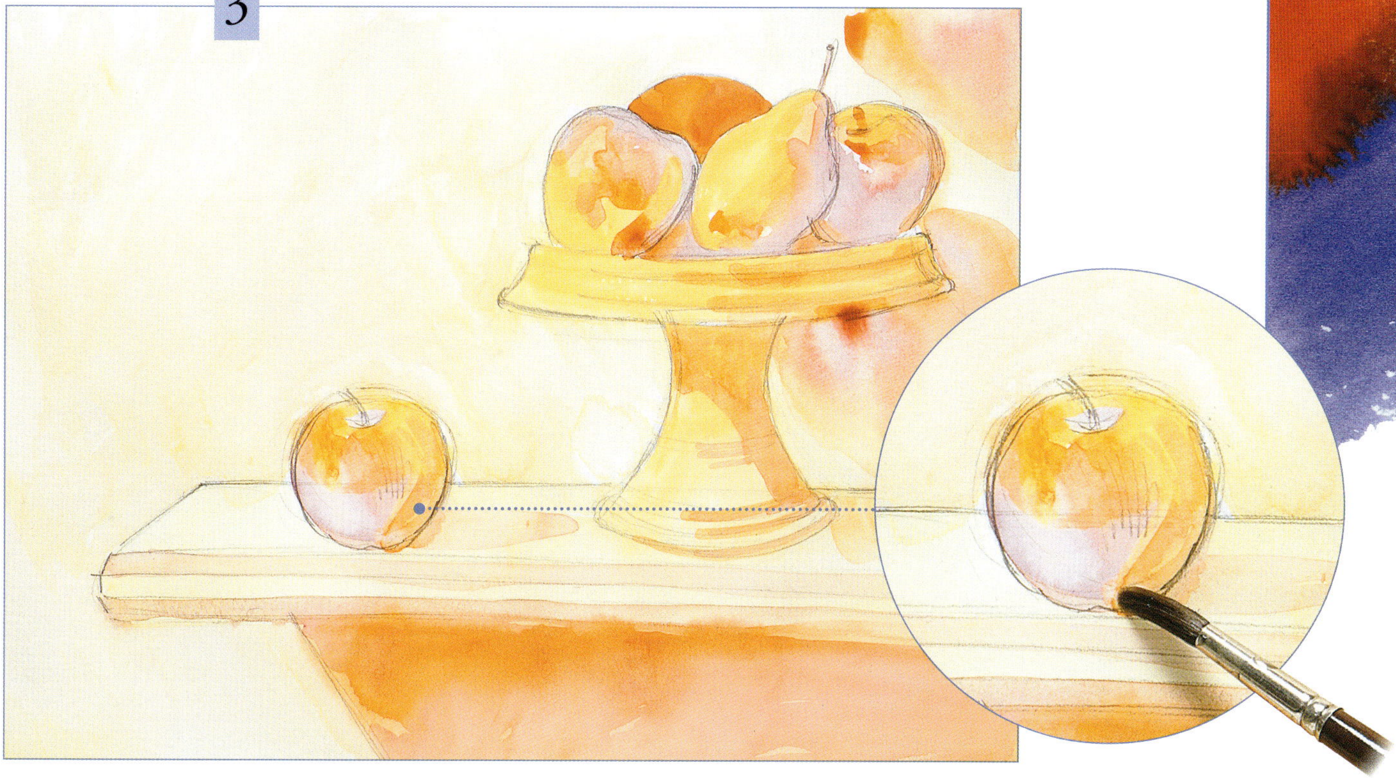

Now it is magenta's turn. We finish covering the white areas of the fruit with a brush charged with paint and a lot of water. The magenta is applied as a glaze over the orange shadows when they are still damp.

The colour applications are light, made in a single pass without much pressure on the brush; otherwise we would smear the colour that is underneath.

4

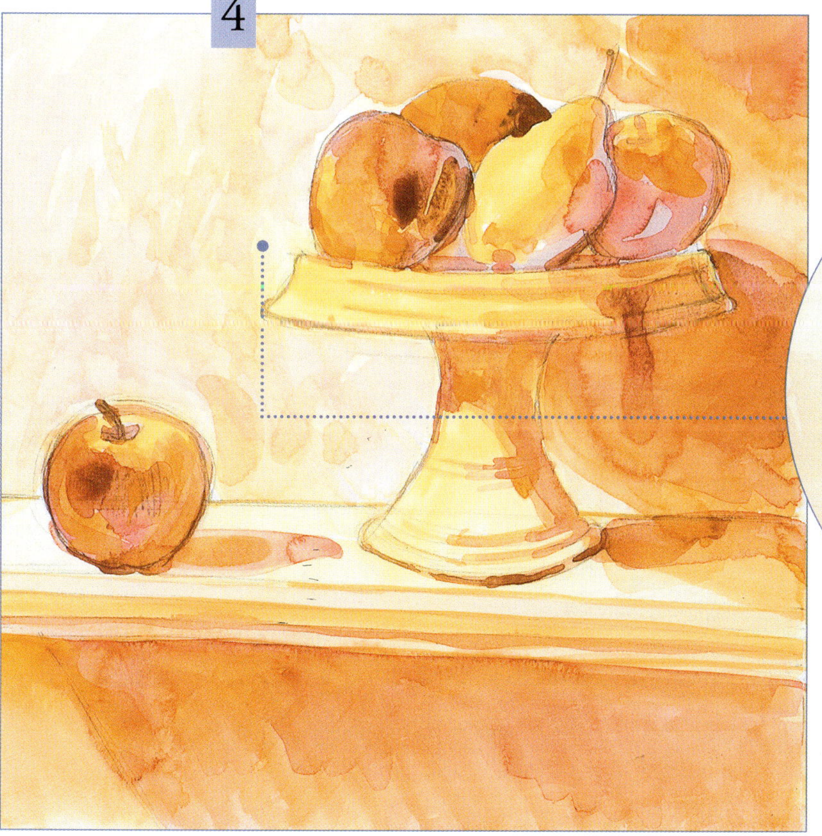

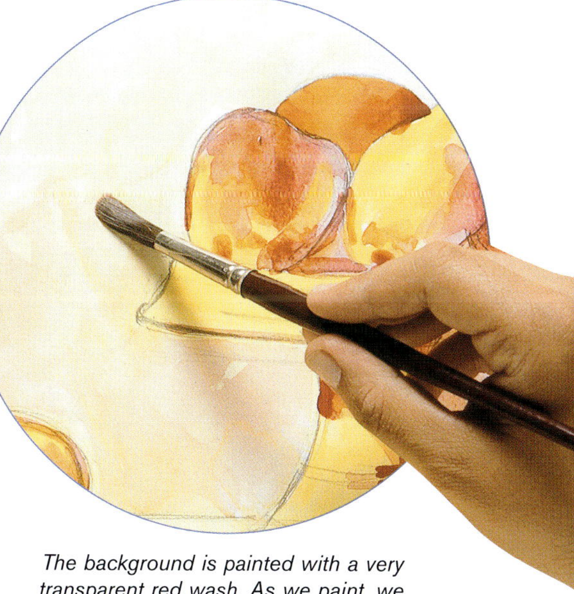

The background is painted with a very transparent red wash. As we paint, we leave some areas open, allowing the yellow underneath to show through; this will also leave more evidence of the brushstroke.

New brushstrokes of red are laid over the previous ones to intensify the colour of the fruit. The darkest parts of the shadows are painted with sienna mixed with red; the contrast lets the illuminated areas stand out.

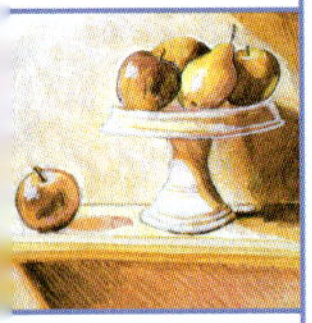

5

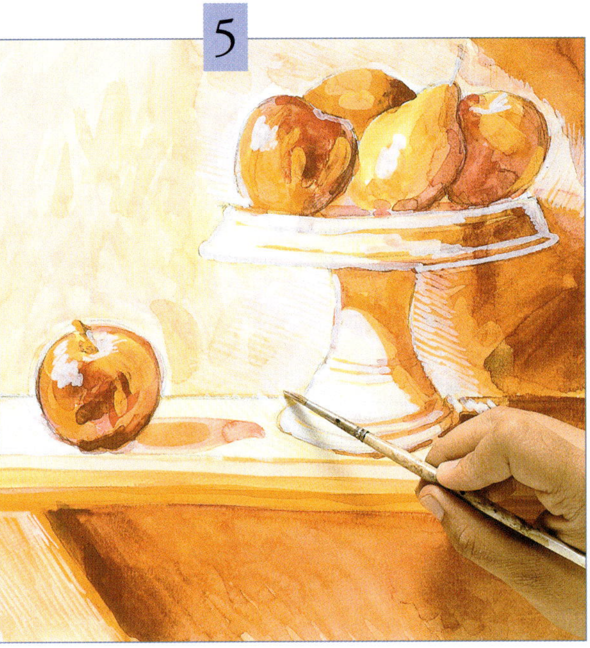

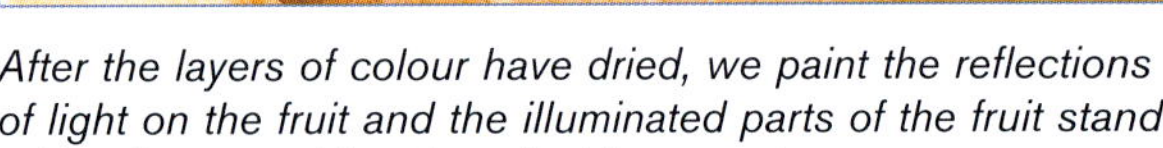

After the layers of colour have dried, we paint the reflections of light on the fruit and the illuminated parts of the fruit stand with a fine round brush and white gouache.

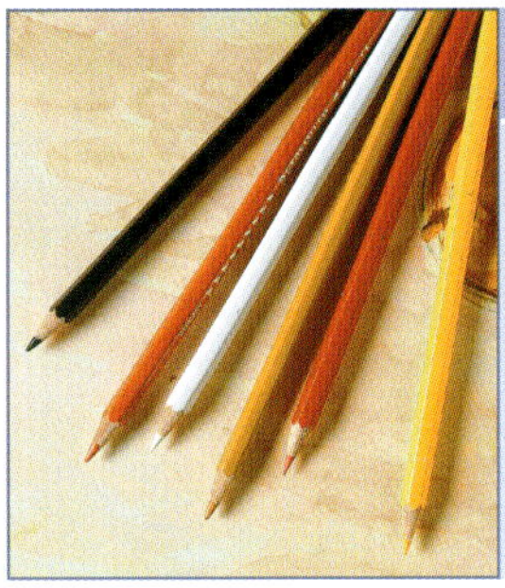

Tip

Coloured pencils are an ideal medium for finishing a work made using washes and brushstrokes. The range used in this exercise consists of only warm colours.

We use a sienna pencil to delineate the contour of the fruit stand, varying the degree of pressure to create the deepest value at the edge.

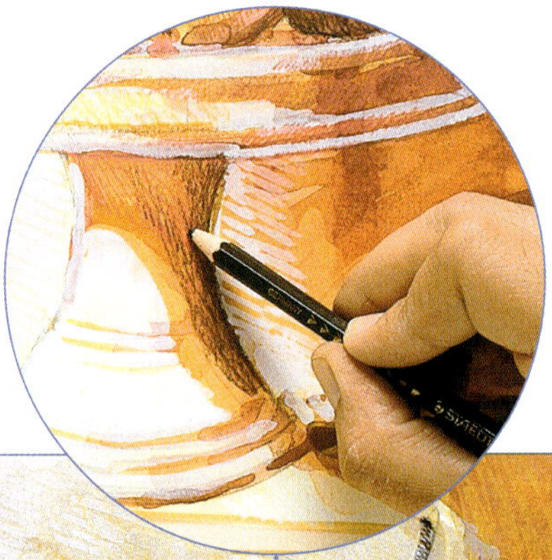

6

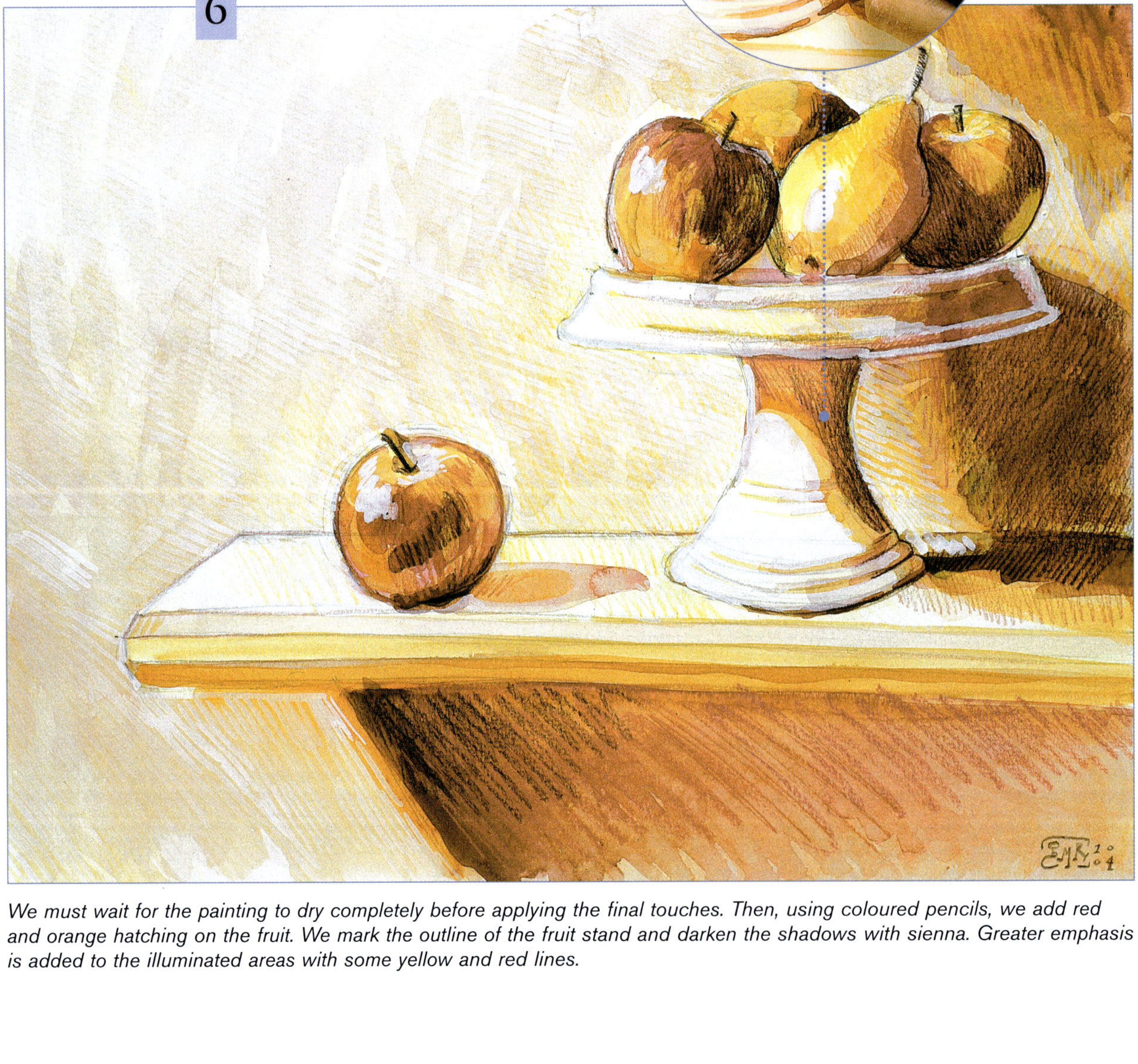

We must wait for the painting to dry completely before applying the final touches. Then, using coloured pencils, we add red and orange hatching on the fruit. We mark the outline of the fruit stand and darken the shadows with sienna. Greater emphasis is added to the illuminated areas with some yellow and red lines.

A PEAR *with* WARM COLOURS

You may have had difficulty understanding how a few brushstrokes of different colours can create the effect of volume in a painting of fruit. In this section, we present a brief study that shows the pictorial evolution of a piece of fruit treated individually. It demonstrates how each new layer of colour is essential for creating tonal gradations in the form of the fruit and constructing its volume.

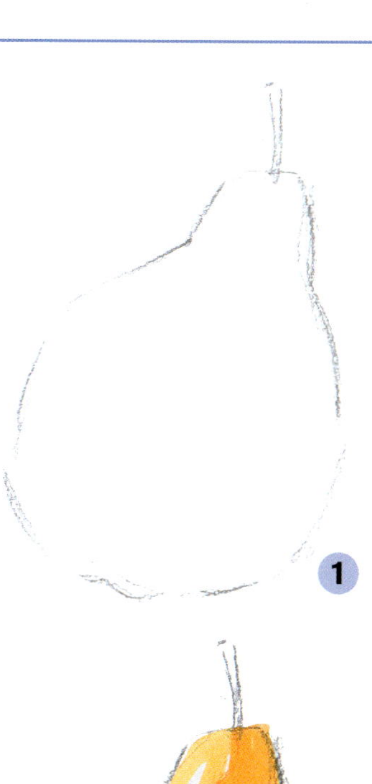

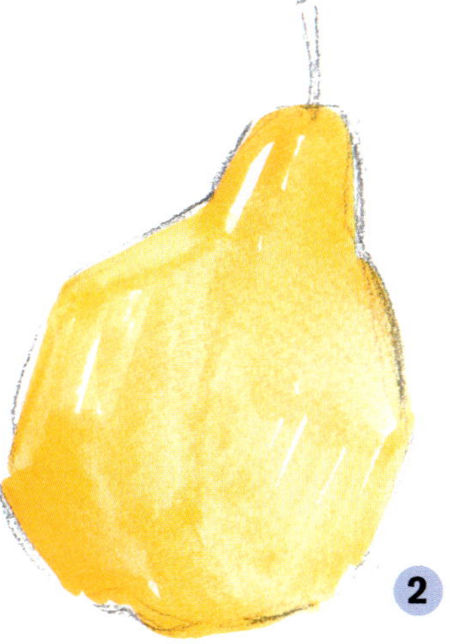

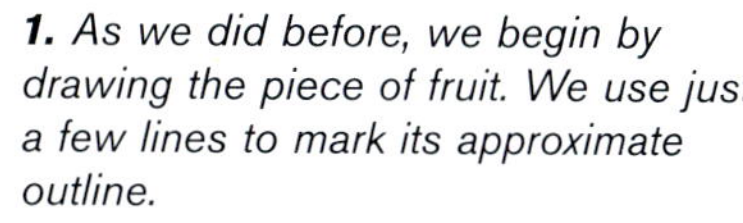

__1.__ As we did before, we begin by drawing the piece of fruit. We use just a few lines to mark its approximate outline.

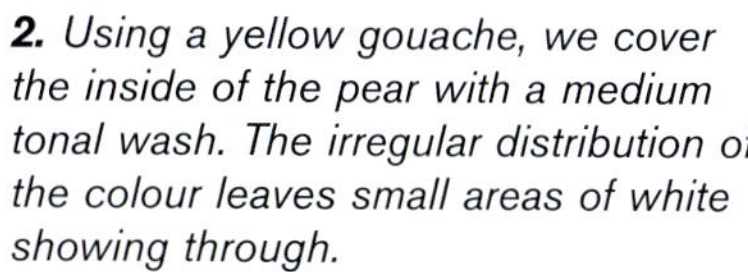

__2.__ Using a yellow gouache, we cover the inside of the pear with a medium tonal wash. The irregular distribution of the colour leaves small areas of white showing through.

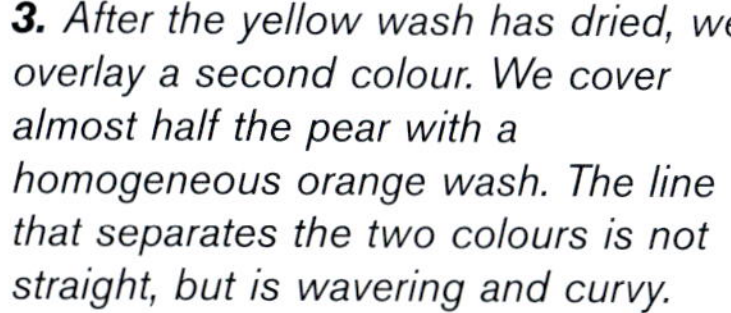

__3.__ After the yellow wash has dried, we overlay a second colour. We cover almost half the pear with a homogeneous orange wash. The line that separates the two colours is not straight, but is wavering and curvy.

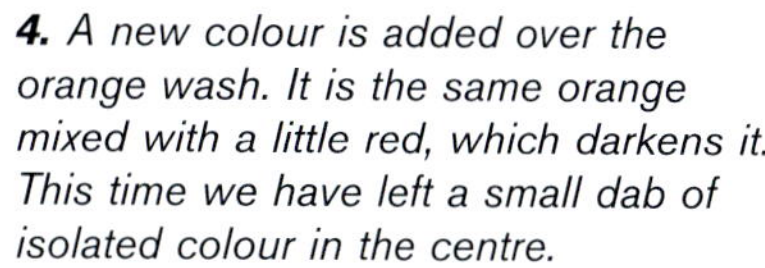

__4.__ A new colour is added over the orange wash. It is the same orange mixed with a little red, which darkens it. This time we have left a small dab of isolated colour in the centre.

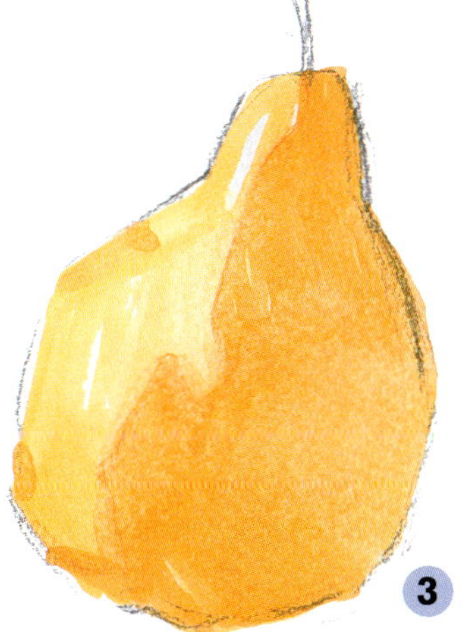

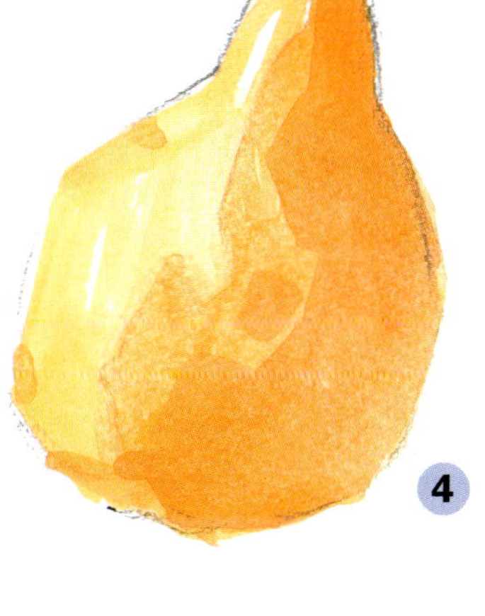

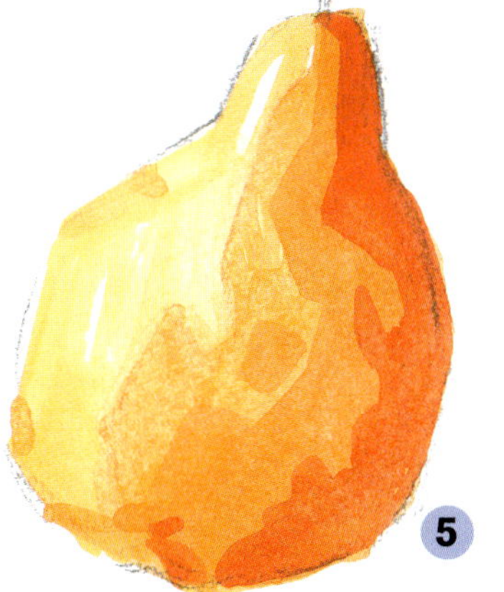

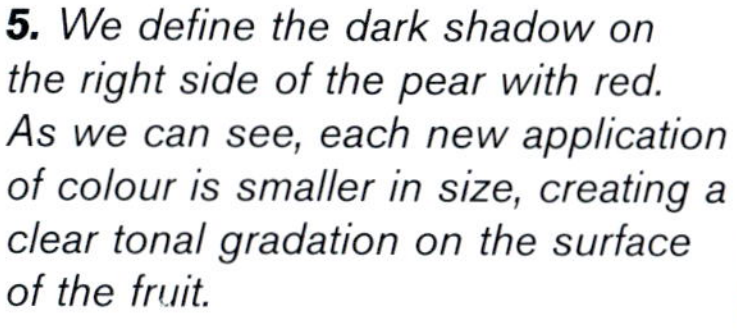

__5.__ We define the dark shadow on the right side of the pear with red. As we can see, each new application of colour is smaller in size, creating a clear tonal gradation on the surface of the fruit.

__6.__ We then do the final retouching with coloured pencils. They are used to recapture the outline, and we add some lines to the layers of orange colour.

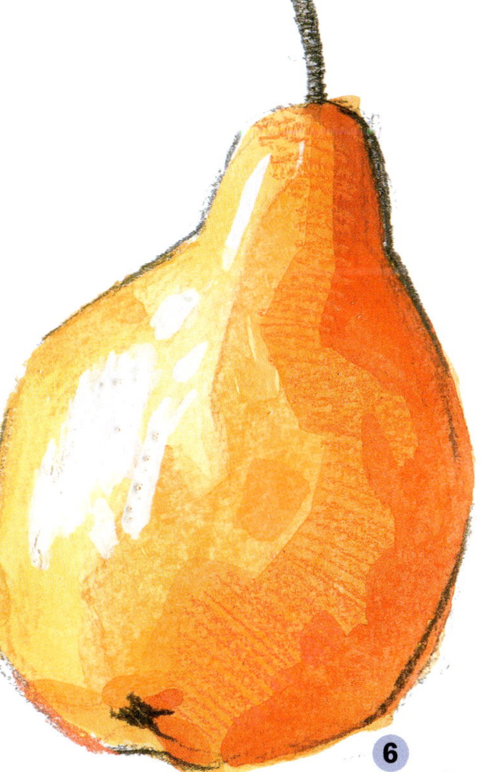

The Impact of COLOUR

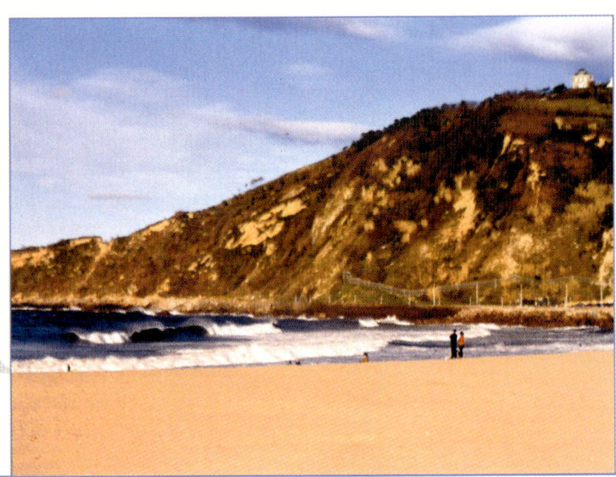

This exercise does not focus so much on the expressiveness of colour in its maximum level of saturation as it does on studying how it impacts the canvas, with the expansiveness, gesture and immediacy of large areas of colour that heighten the chromatic effect. This treatment is often used when working in an area between figural work and abstraction.

We will try to paint a coastal landscape using the collage technique with neutral colours (not very saturated and somewhat greyed). Oil paint is the best medium for working with the impasto and controlling the thickness and direction of the brushstrokes.

1

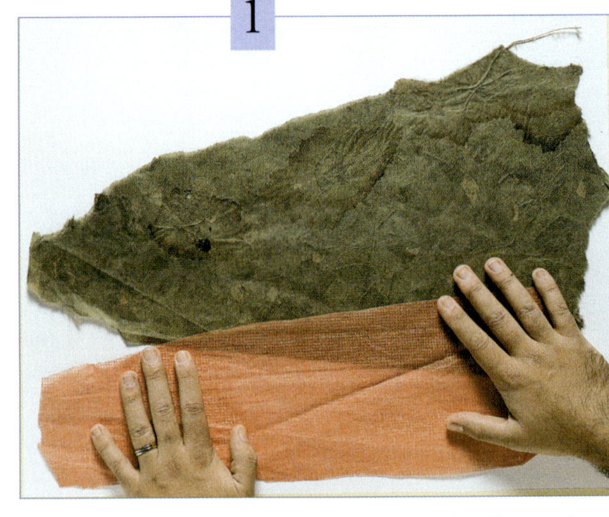

We approximate the model with two areas of uniform colour indicating the hill and the beach. These are represented by two pieces of paper with different textures and colours, which are slightly overlapped on the canvas until a convincing composition is found.

2

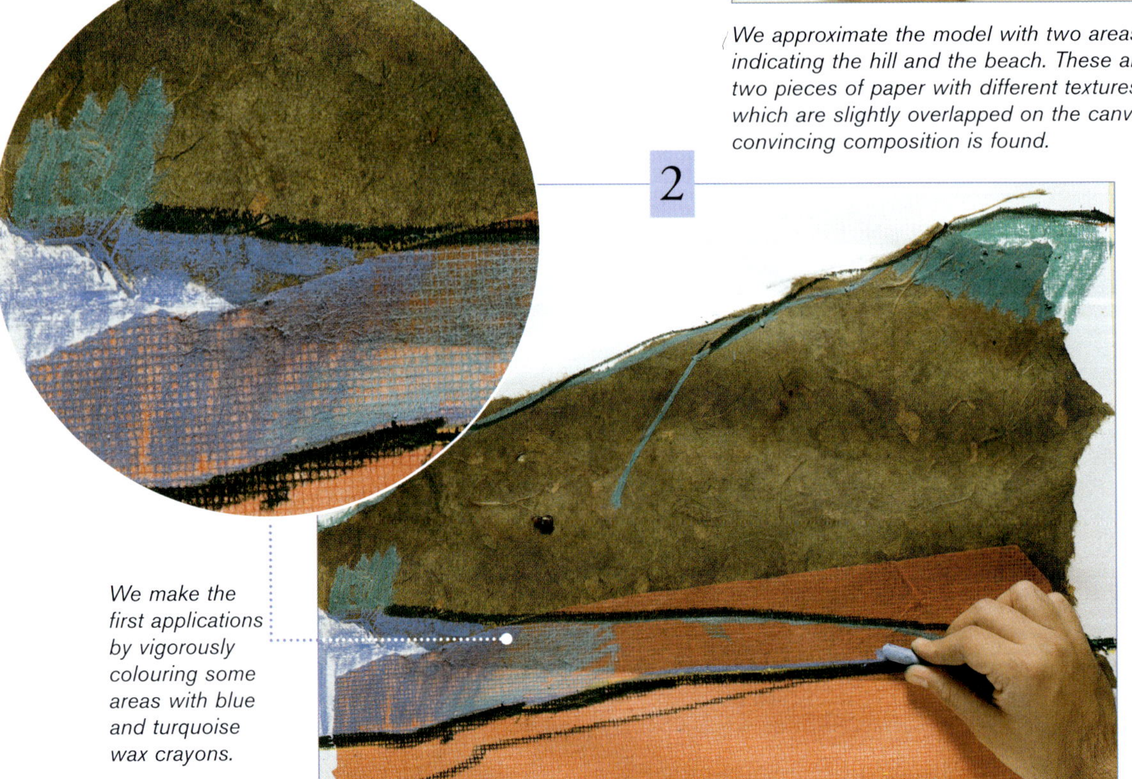

The next step is to attach the paper to the canvas with a clean brush and glue. After allowing the adhesive to dry for half an hour, we draw the outlines of the landscape, making wide bold lines with wax crayons of different colours.

We make the first applications by vigorously colouring some areas with blue and turquoise wax crayons.

3

Using a wide bristle brush, we paint the sky with wide strokes of blue diluted with turpentine. We paint the same blue, much lightened with white, over the previous blue. To counteract the purity of the white, it is a good idea to use a slightly dirty turpentine.

Working with the same flat wide brush, we add different values of green to the brown paper that will act as the hill in the background. It is a good idea not to completely cover the background so that both colours will interact to form a range of neutral colours (greyish and brownish greens).

4

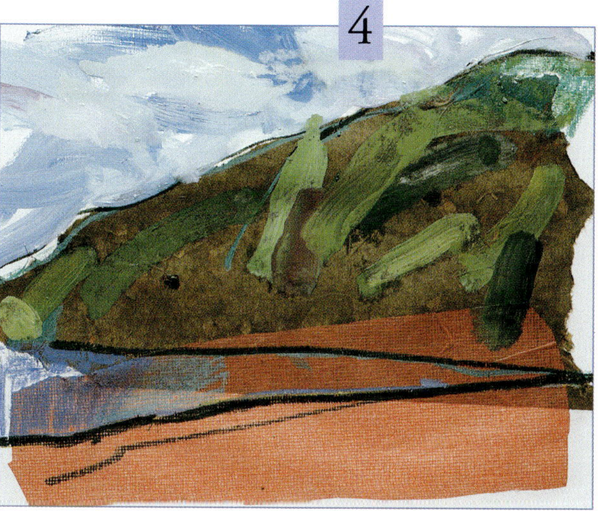

To differentiate the background from the foreground, which is the beach, we will use another range of neutral colours with value contrasts, since the foreground has lighter colours. Beginning with ochre, we reduce its saturation by mixing it with white and again adding a large amount of dirty turpentine.

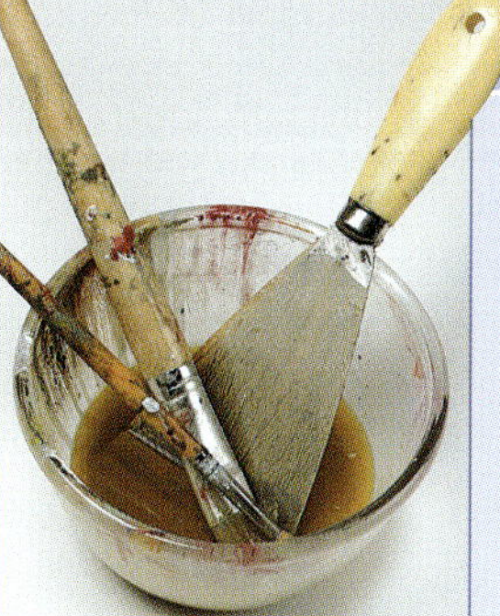

Tip

A good trick for making neutral colours is to work with very dirty turpentine. Adding a bit of turpentine to each colour mixture will make it a little grey and muddy, creating a neutral colour by reducing its brightness and purity.

5

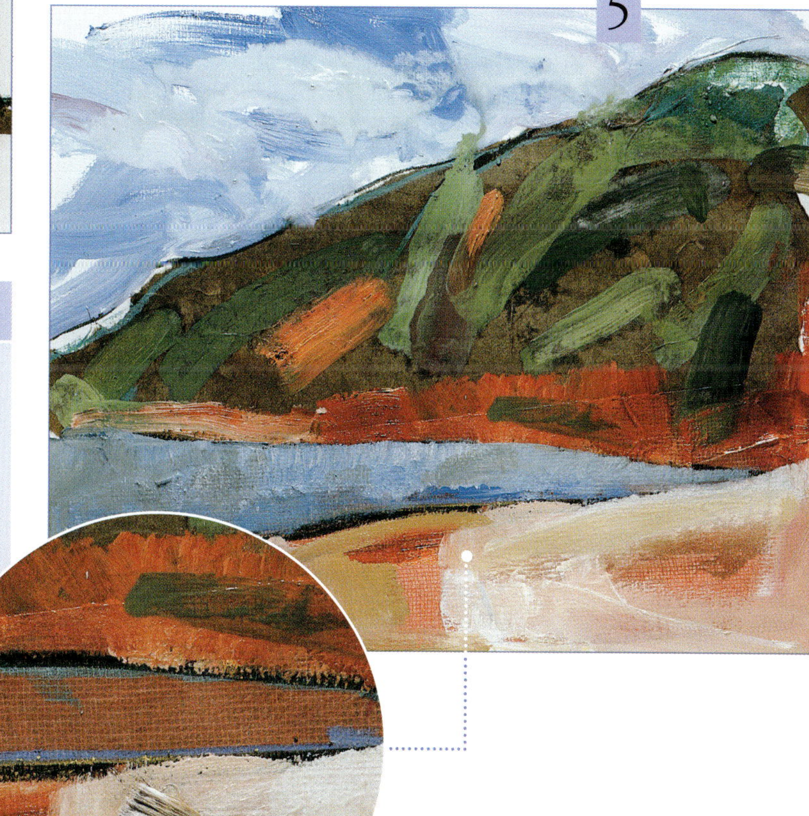

We paint the foreground using a medium flat brush. The paint is mixed with a lot of turpentine and applied thickly, but without completely covering the reddish paper that is underneath.

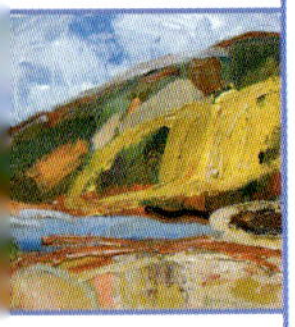

6

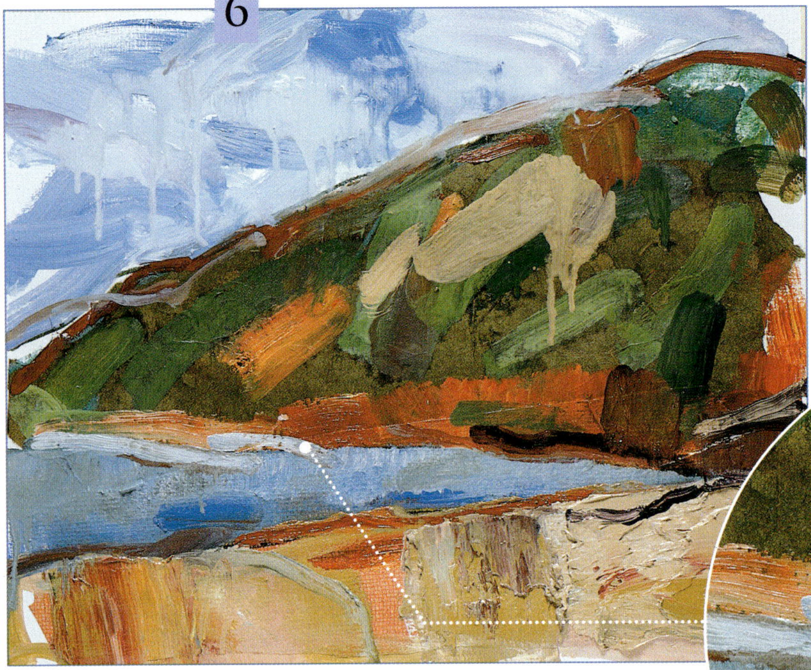

As we work, it is possible to lose the initial structure. It is a good idea to reinforce it with new lines made with a fine round brush, which softens the transition between two strongly contrasting colours like the blue of the sea and the red of the hill.

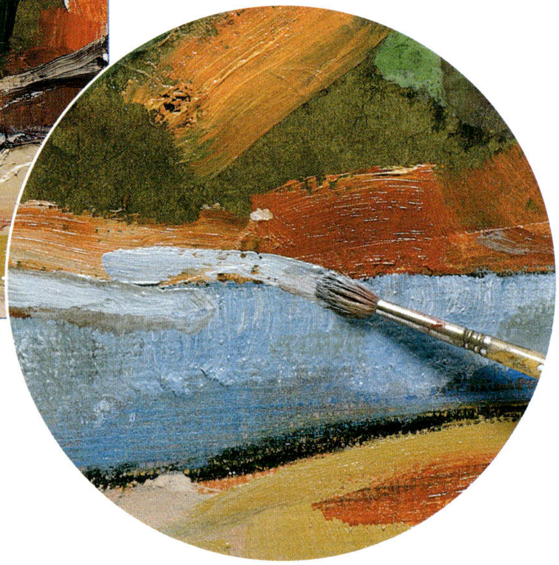

New diluted brushstrokes are added to the previous ones, causing puddles of diluted paint. Since the colour is very runny we tip the canvas to make it run, adding expressiveness and fluidity to the work. The beach area is finished with thick heavy paint in mixed ochre, white, pink, and carmine, applied with an industrial spatula.

7

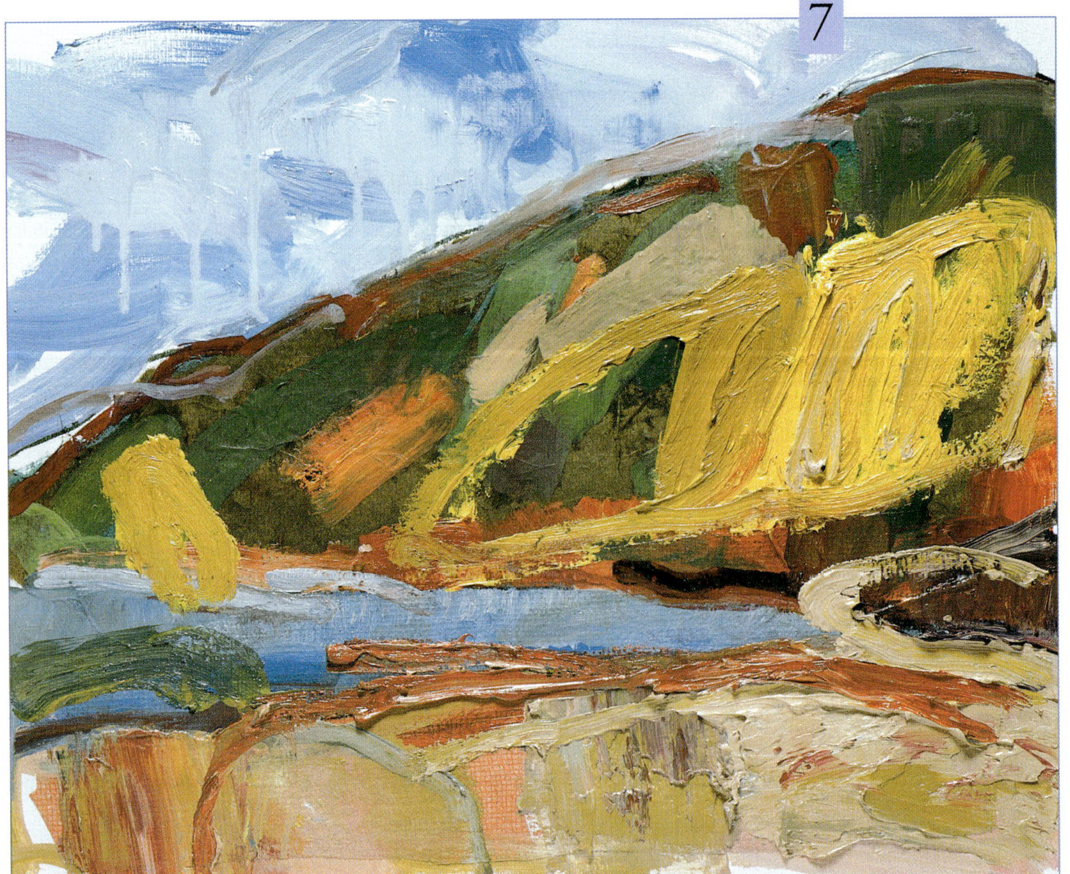

We could consider the exercise finished with the previous step, but to take the composition to a more abstract and expressive direction, we finish it by applying a heavy yellow impasto that covers the green background. The yellowish form is vague and has no relation to the real subject, but as a bright and luminous colour it acts as the focal point of the painting. We do the same thing along the line of the beach with the brush charged with red.

An INFORMAL TREATMENT

In the previous exercise, the colours have been constructed in quite an informal manner, and many effects on the canvas are rough or seem to be uncontrolled. The abundance of dirty turpentine makes the colours greyish and runny, allowing them to harmonize with each other and the brush to flow easily across the surface of the canvas. Let's study some of the effects separately.

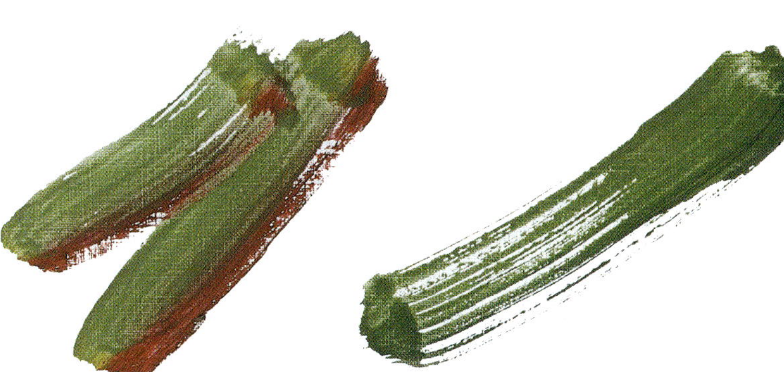

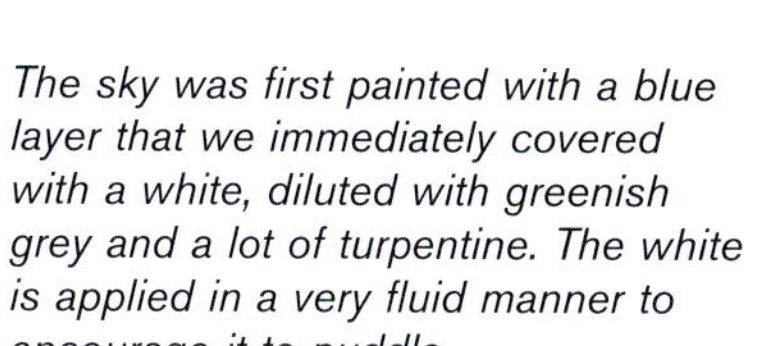

The sky was first painted with a blue layer that we immediately covered with a white, diluted with greenish grey and a lot of turpentine. The white is applied in a very fluid manner to encourage it to puddle.

We applied greenish brushstrokes on the brown paper. If we do not mix the colours thoroughly on the palette, we get brushstrokes showing several colours in the same line.

If we brush across a dry area of the canvas, the line becomes streaked, that is, it shows marks of the bristles of the brush.

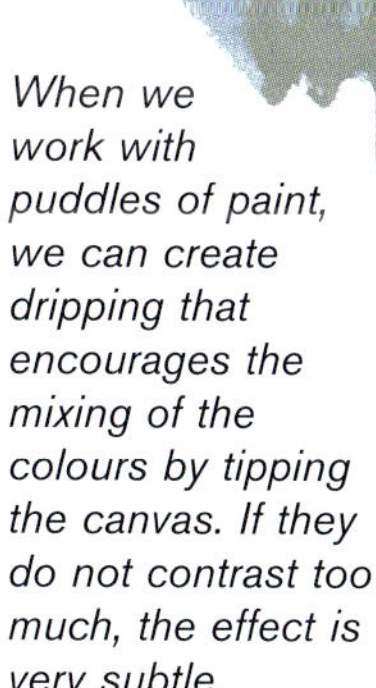

When we work with puddles of paint, we can create dripping that encourages the mixing of the colours by tipping the canvas. If they do not contrast too much, the effect is very subtle.

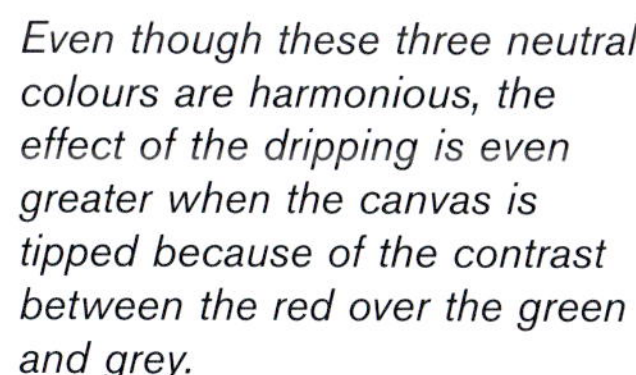

Even though these three neutral colours are harmonious, the effect of the dripping is even greater when the canvas is tipped because of the contrast between the red over the green and grey.

Lines are added right where two areas of colour meet to reduce the contrast. This can be done by slightly inclining the brush and rotating the point while moving it along the surface of the painting. This way we take full advantage of the colour.

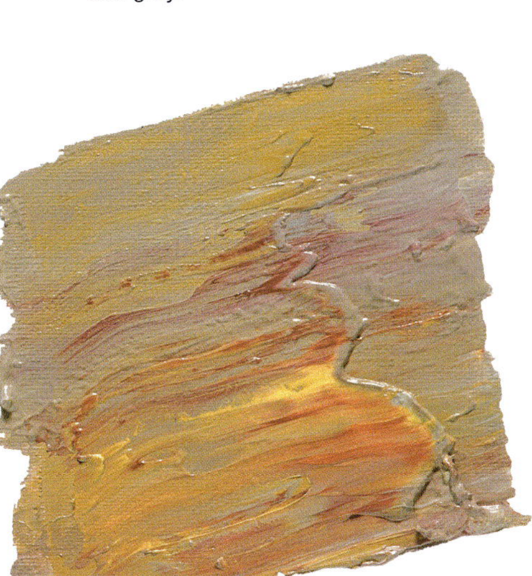

The last additions of colour are applied as impastos. Warm colours are mixed on the palette and then applied heavily on the canvas. This reduces the brightness of the red and the yellow and better integrates them into the painting.

Blocks of COLOUR

LANDSCAPE *with* *Blocks of* COLOUR

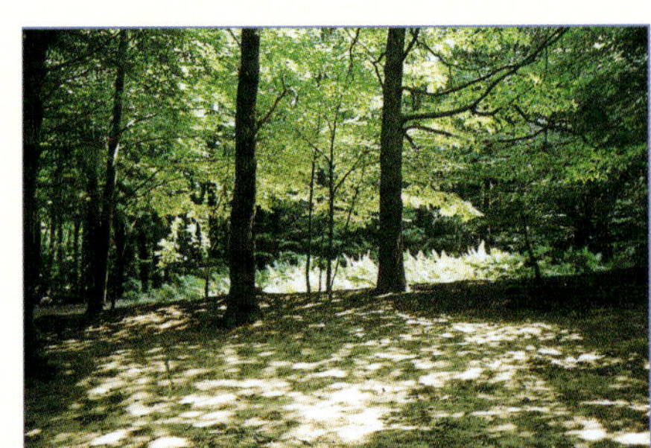

The following example is painted with blocks of colour, that is with small and individual strokes of colour applied directly to the canvas. Working on the surface with dense and saturated colours tends to emphasize the contrasts; lines made up of individual brush-strokes become large areas of colour with vibrant effects. We use oil paint because of its covering power and its creamy texture.

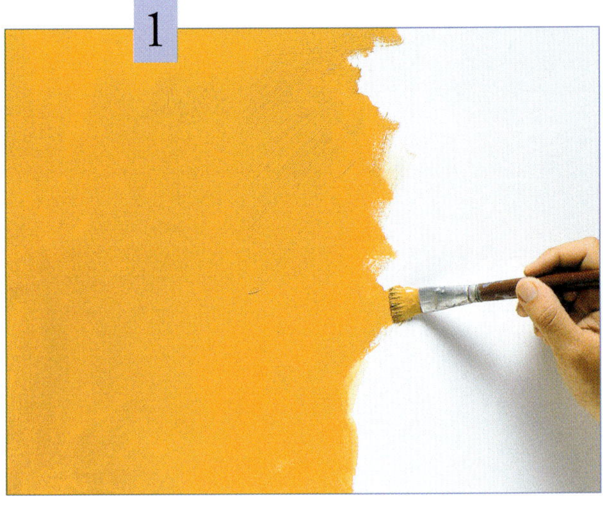

1

It is best to use dabs of colour on a background that has previously been painted with a colour. We cover the support with yellow ochre, using acrylic paint instead of oil because of its fast drying time.

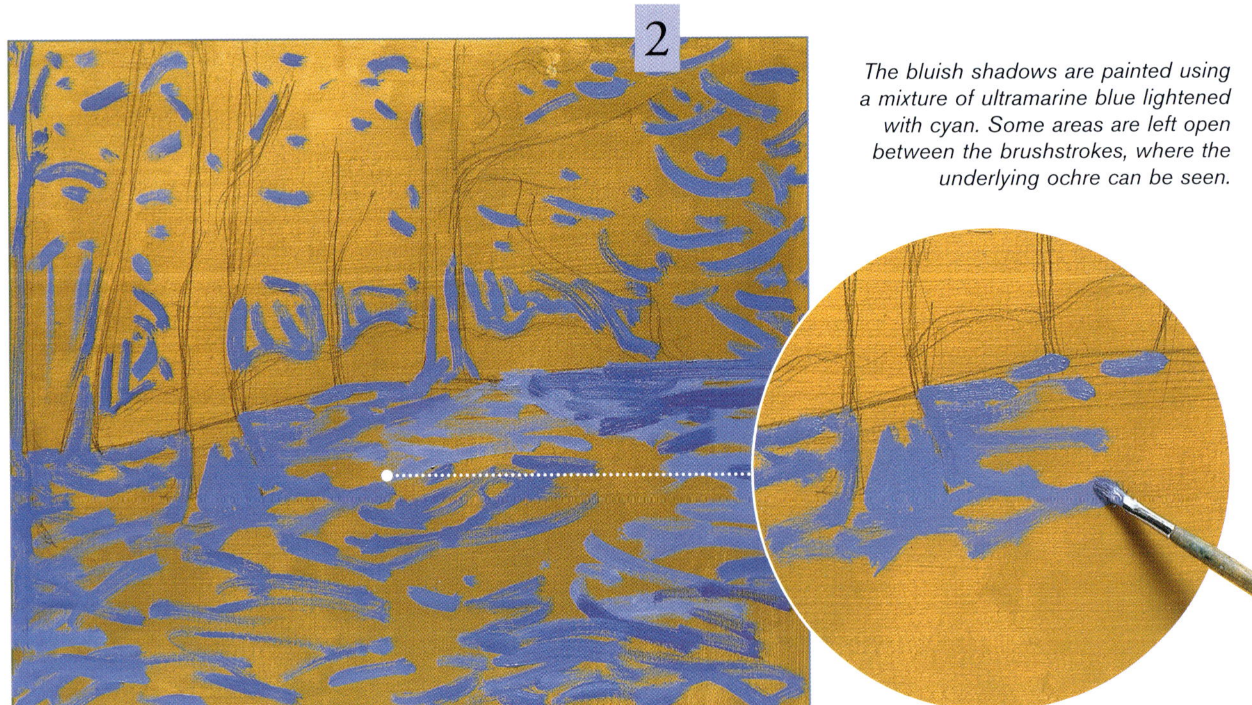

2

The bluish shadows are painted using a mixture of ultramarine blue lightened with cyan. Some areas are left open between the brushstrokes, where the underlying ochre can be seen.

After about twenty minutes, the first layer of colour has dried and we can sketch the subject with an HB pencil. We paint the shadows first in blue and covering a large part of the forest floor. We add a few strokes of colour to the foliage of the trees.

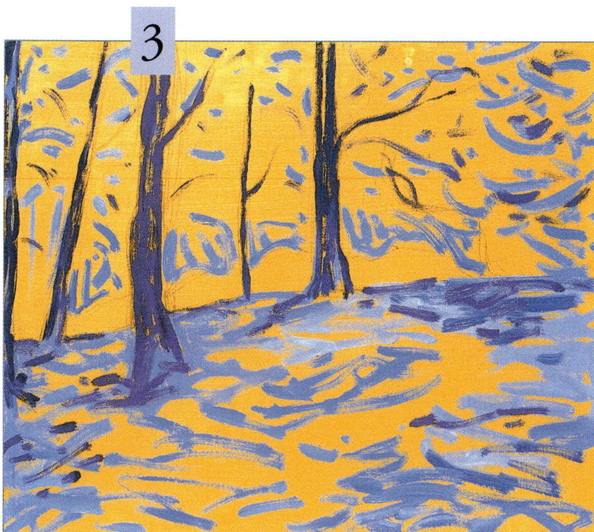

We now show the darkest parts of the painting. The trunks of the nearest trees are painted with violet. The brushstrokes do not form a mass of compact colour, but leave open areas where the background colour shows through, like the forest floor.

The first contrasts of light and shadow appear among the leaves on the ground. Flashes of yellow mixed with white stand out on a blanket of blue brushstrokes.

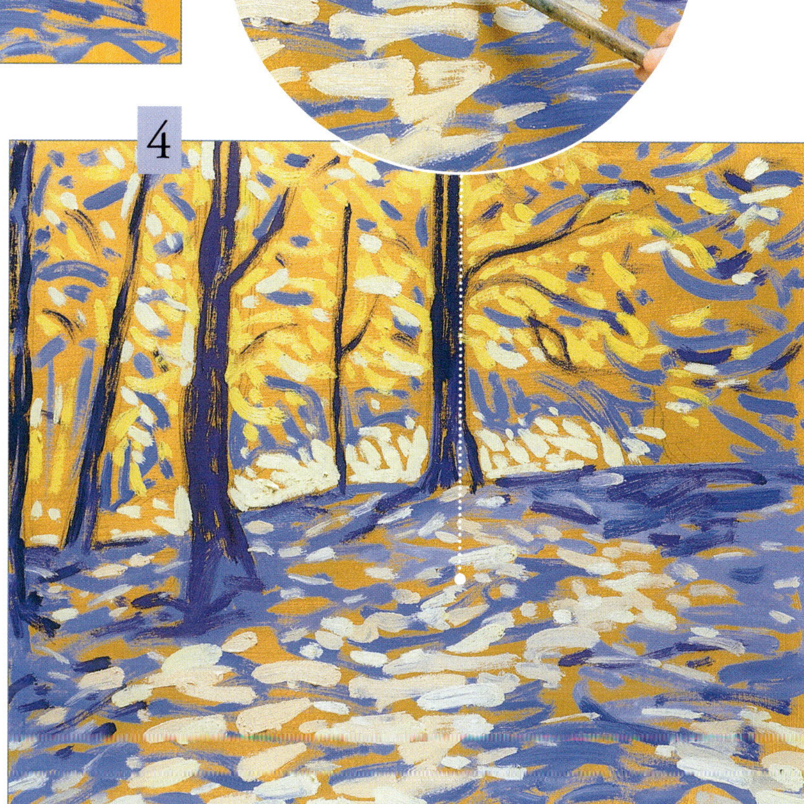

We paint the flashes of light on the ground in a mixture of yellow and white and a yellowish pink. In the background we combine the light yellow with brushstrokes of a more saturated yellow in the foliage of the trees.

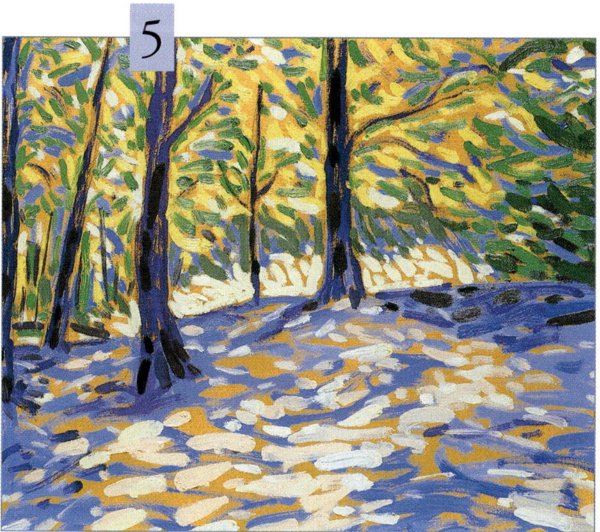

Over the yellow that represents the leaves illuminated by the light of the sun, we apply new dabs of a medium green and a darker green in the more shaded areas. The green over the still-fresh yellow should be applied with a single stroke; otherwise we would lift the colour underneath and both colours would become uncontrollably mixed.

Tip

Before attempting a colourful subject like this one, it is a good idea to be sure of our intentions concerning colour so we can impart movement and dynamism to the painting.

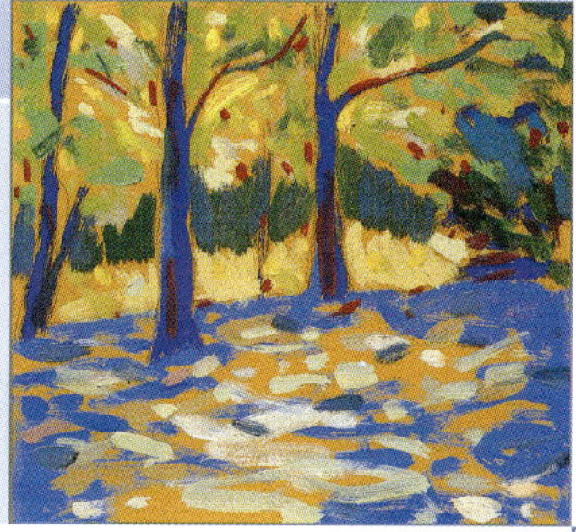

In a loose but controlled manner, we apply dabs of saturated cadmium red in the branches of the trees and a few more on the forest floor. Although this colour does not appear in the real subject, its use adds vividness and warmth to the picture.

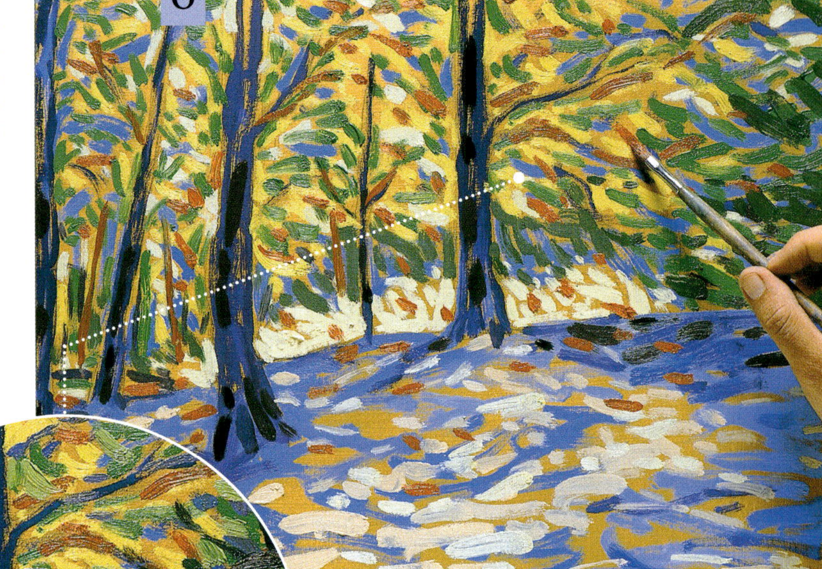

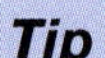

It is not a matter of just applying the brushstrokes – it is important to pay attention to the direction of the lines. They should be horizontal on the ground, vertical on the tree trunks, and expansive on the foliage.

Tip

When applying short brushstrokes of colour, it is enough to touch the brush a single time to the painting. It is an error to dab it several times, since the new colour could become muddy from the underlying colours and we would lose the effect of saturation.

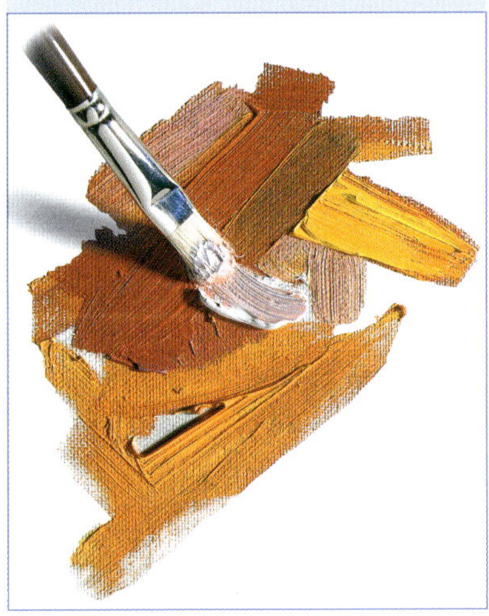

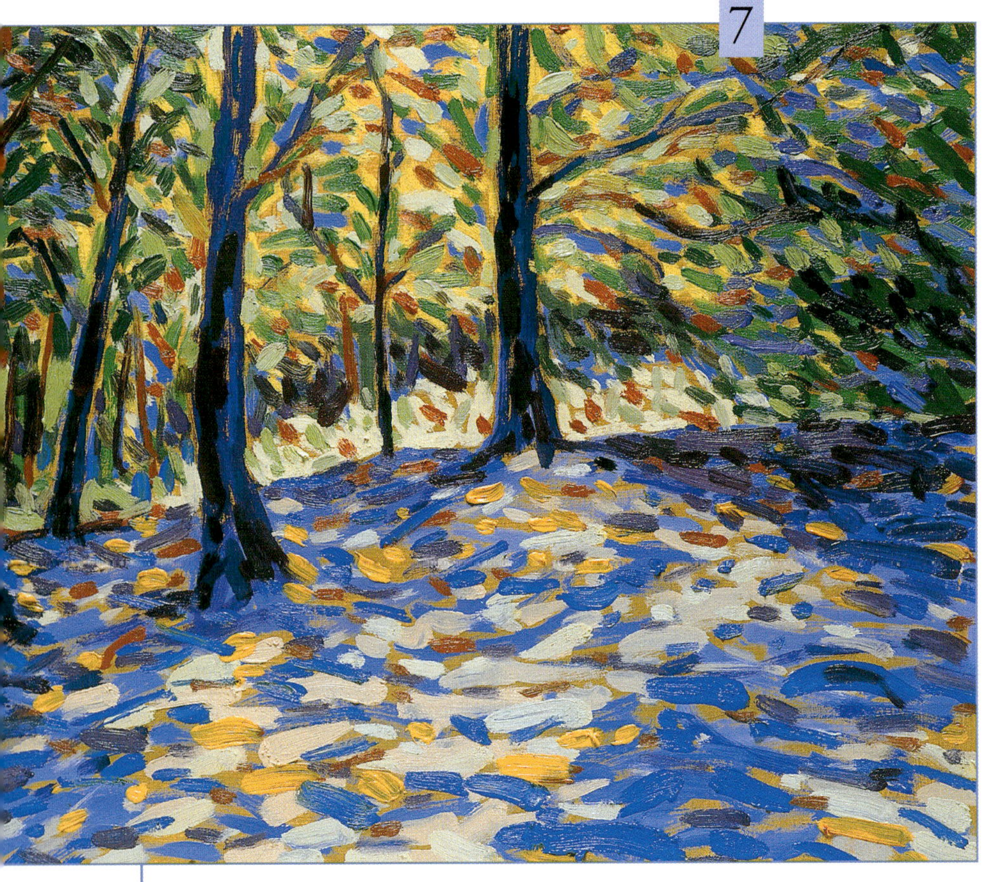

The final result is very vivid because the colours do not cover each other and the intensity of the individual tones is not lost. Not a single part of this painting is flat. The tones and colours are constructed with an intricate web of short brush-strokes reminiscent of the Impressionist painters.

BROKEN COLOUR *and* OPTICAL MIXTURES

As you know, the expression "broken colour" refers to any area of colour that is not completely uniform and covers a wide range of painting effects and techniques. These dabs of colour are generally used with opaque media, and to a lesser extent with watercolour. Let's look at a sample of this.

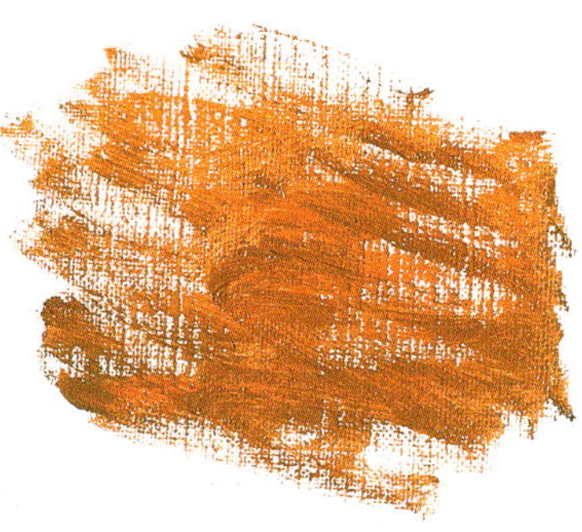

Working with a charge of barely diluted colour, we are able to create an area of colour formed by rough brushstrokes that allow the texture of the canvas to show through.

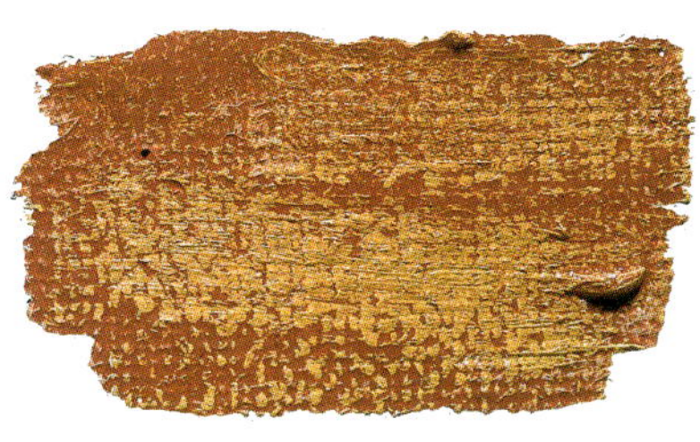

This effect is the result of applying some colour, allowing it to dry, and then applying another brushstroke of undiluted colour over it. The granulated ochre colour allows the red of the background to show through.

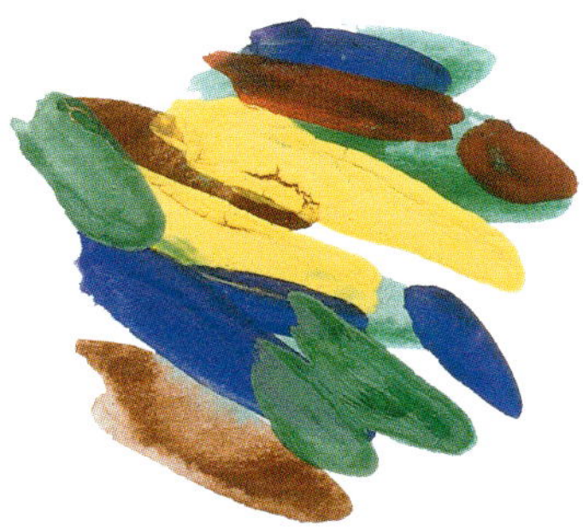

One of the most common effects of the broken colour technique is the overlaying of short opaque brushstrokes that, through optical mixing, enliven the surface of the painting.

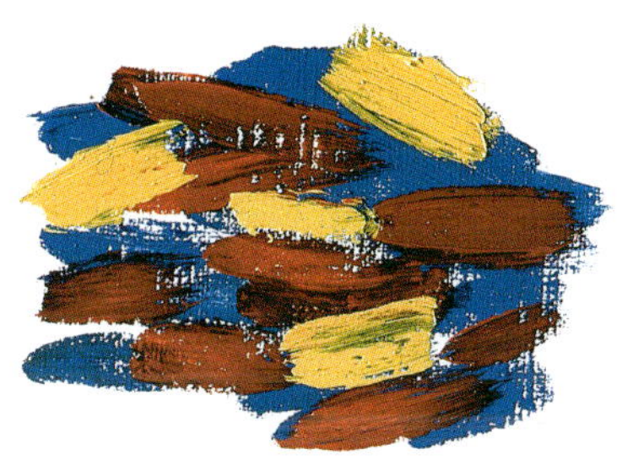

When the brushstrokes are applied dry, the edges of the colours are more defined. If we make two or three passes with the brush instead of one, the colour will mix with the one under it.

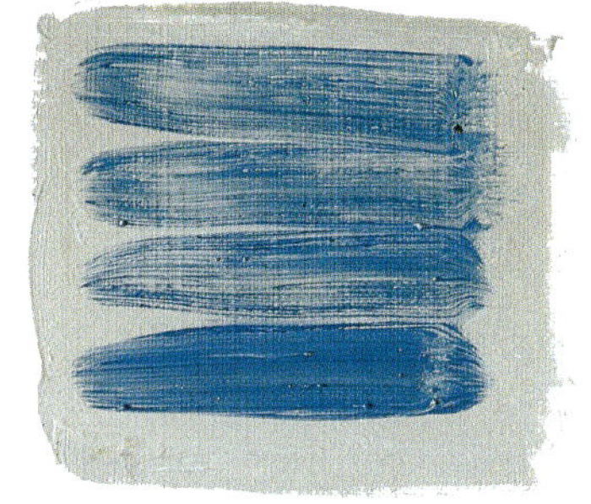

When the lower layer of colour is very damp and we apply a somewhat diluted application, we get striated brushstrokes.

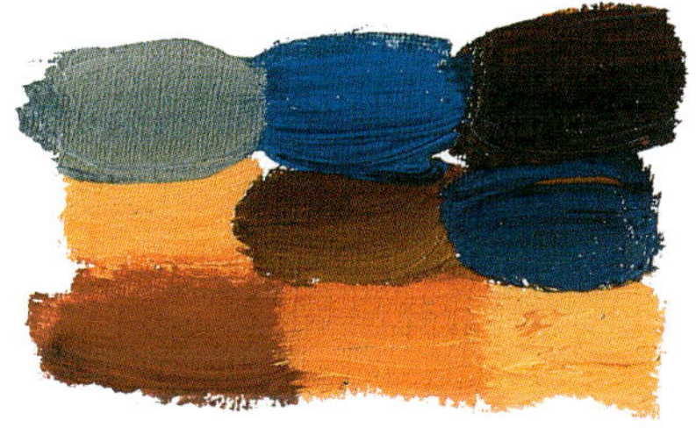

Broken colour can also be applied by combining uniformly arranged brushstrokes that are juxtaposed without any mixing at all.

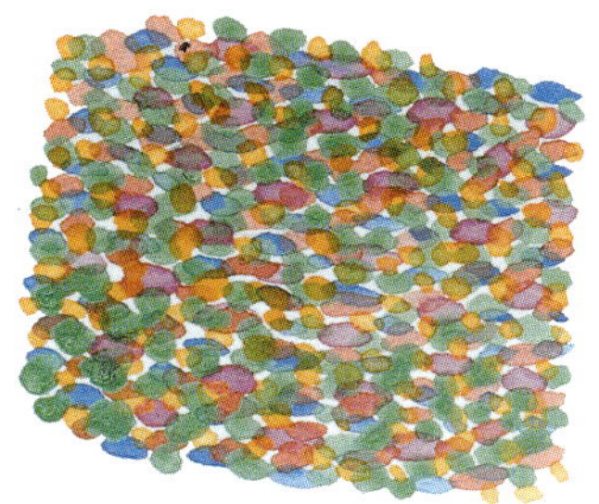

Pointillism is one of the best-known optical mixing effects.

In the "wet white" technique, the ground of the painting is prepared with a layer of thick white paint.

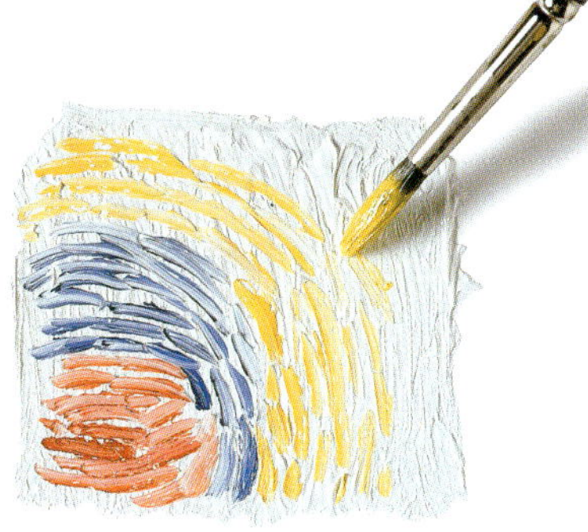

Then we cover the white with quick small brushstrokes of saturated colour. The colours will mix with the white and take on light pastel tones.

Complementary COLOURS

Still Life with Complementary COLOURS

There are many ways to create a colourful and original painting. The combination of strong contrasts between complementary colours on the same canvas is a much used method. It is a matter of painting the objects and the most well-lit areas of drapery with pure and lively colours like orange, red and yellow. Then the shadows that they project are resolved with applications of complementary colours, thus creating a very violent contrast. In the following case, the medium we use is acrylic paint.

1

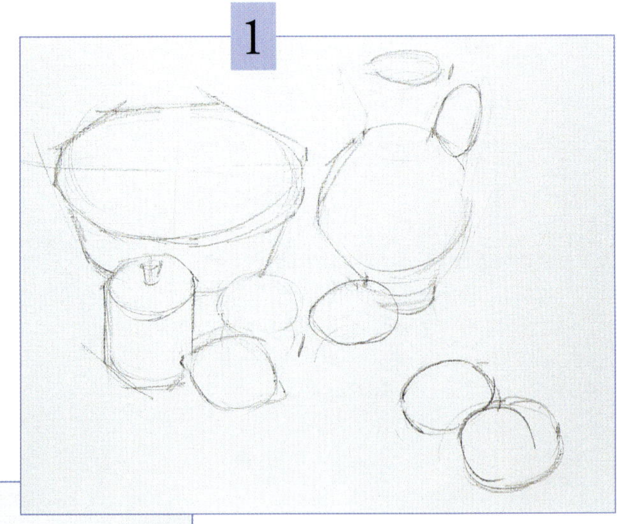

The initial drawing is very simple. We hardly spend any time on it, since it will soon be painted over. It is composed of a few circles that indicate the pitcher and the fruit. The sugar bowl is drawn with a cylindrical form, and an oval is enough to represent the lid of the basket.

2

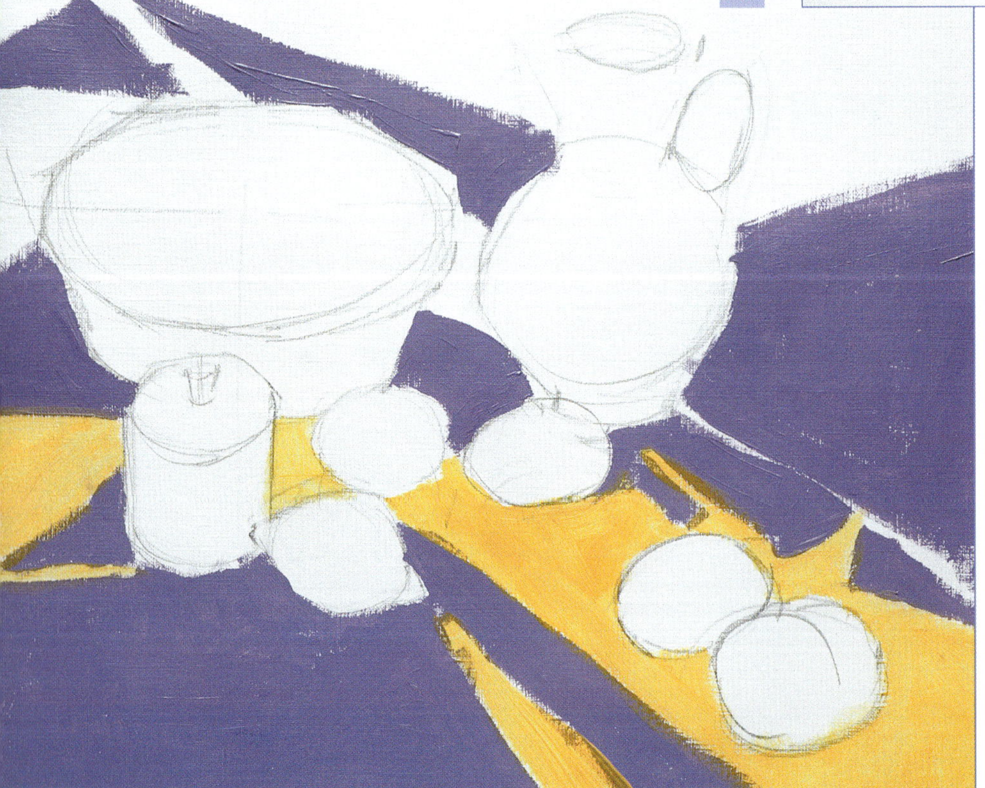

Using a thick, round bristle brush, we approximate the illuminated parts of the fabric with saturated yellow. We are aware that in the real subject the fabric is blue, but we are playing with the colours. Looking for a vivid contrast, we paint the shaded areas of the drapery with yellow's complementary colour – a bright medium violet is the most appropriate.

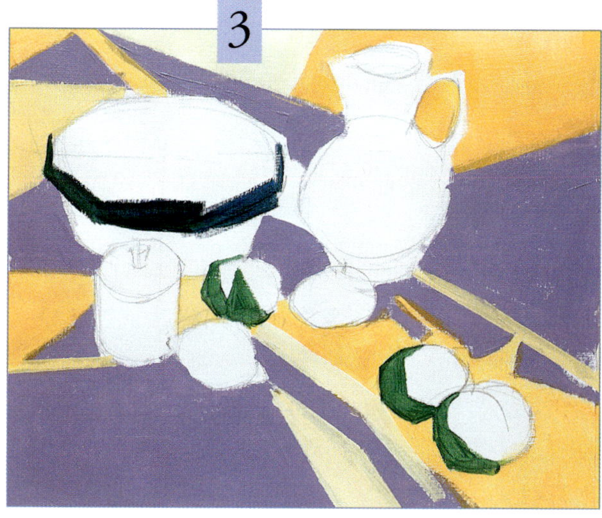

The background has been covered with strong contrasts created by the complementary colours violet and yellow. We apply areas of a lightened yellow in some spaces to soften the effect of the contrast, since the less saturated the colour, the softer the contrast. The shadows on the apples are painted green and the edge of the lid of the basket is painted a dark blue green.

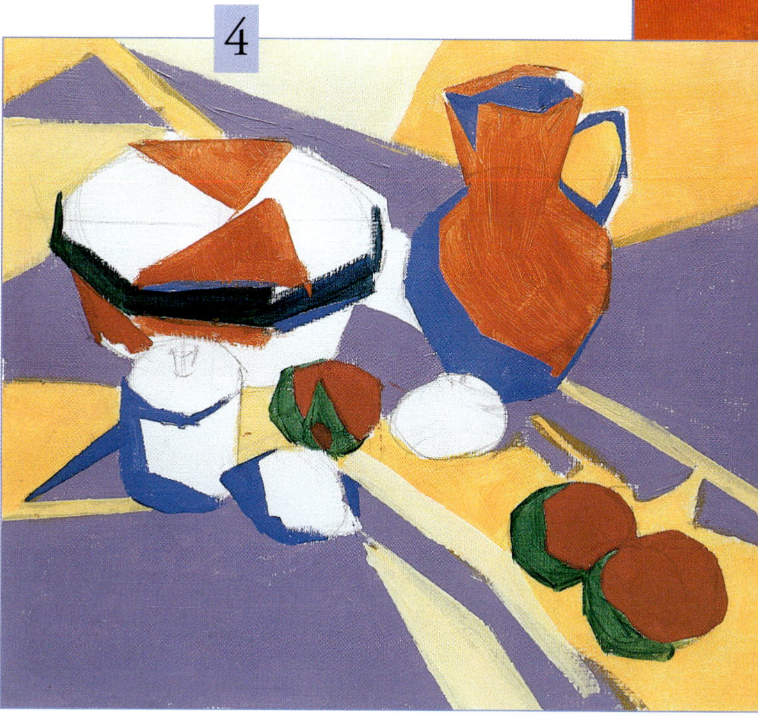

We paint the shadows of the rest of the objects, this time with a blue colour on the left side of the pitcher, the sugar bowl and the lemons. Based on the colours of the shadows, we paint the illuminated parts of the objects with the complementary colour. Thus, the red of the apples is the opposite of the green shadow and the orange on the jar strongly contrasts with blue.

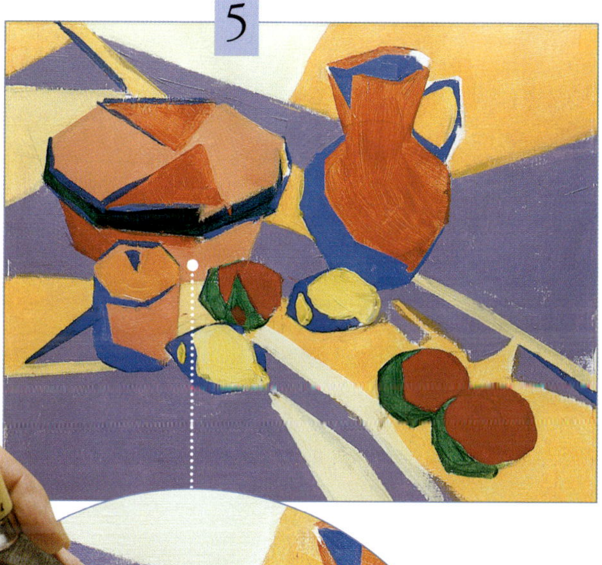

We add new applications of orange to the sugar bowl and the white parts of the lemons are painted with light cadmium yellow. The wicker basket is painted with an orange base colour that is somewhat lightened with a touch of white. On top of this base we paint two geometric shapes with a brighter orange that help explain the form.

Tip

To avoid getting involved in details, reflections, textures and various effects that can distract our attention from the purely chromatic experiment, we apply the colours flat and in the form of geometric shapes.

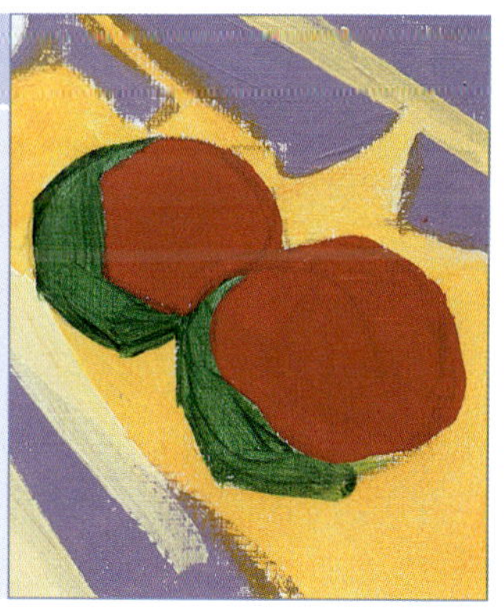

We use a spatula as a template for controlling the straight, striking edges of the flat planes of colour.

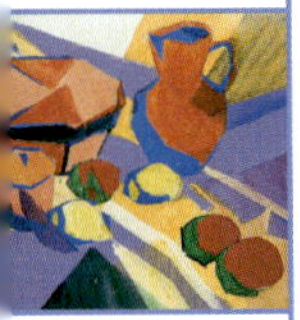

6

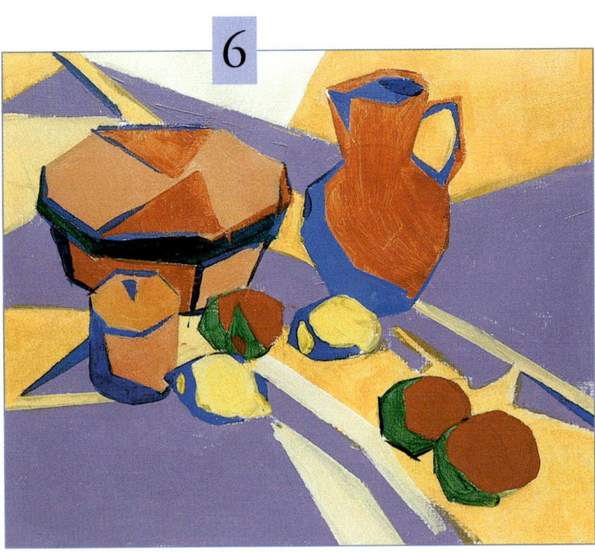

At this point, the exercise is finished. All the objects are composed of a single illuminated part painted in warm saturated colours and a shaded part resolved with the corresponding complementary colours. The result is a very luminous, optimistic and exciting painting.

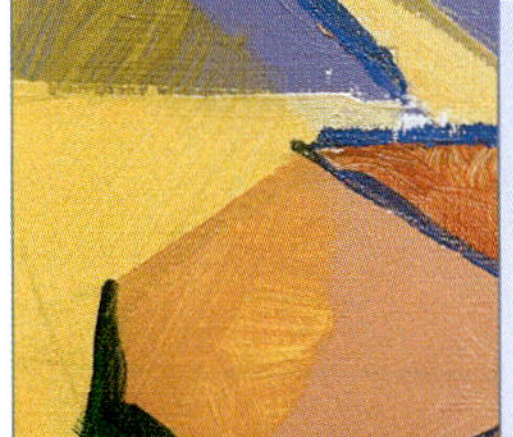

Tip

Glazing produces the opposite effect of contrasting complementary colours; instead of causing colour discord, it tends to unify and even it out. A yellow glaze painted over an area turns the underlying colours toward yellow and causes the values to move closer together.

After letting the painting dry, we will try another interesting chromatic effect: the modification of the underlying colours by glazing. If we wish to reduce the brightness of the colour or the strength of a contrast, we can apply a more or less transparent wash over the area in question to tone down the colour.

The best way to control the geometric shapes when using washes is to cut small card stock templates; they are laid over the surface of the painting to protect the edges of the forms.

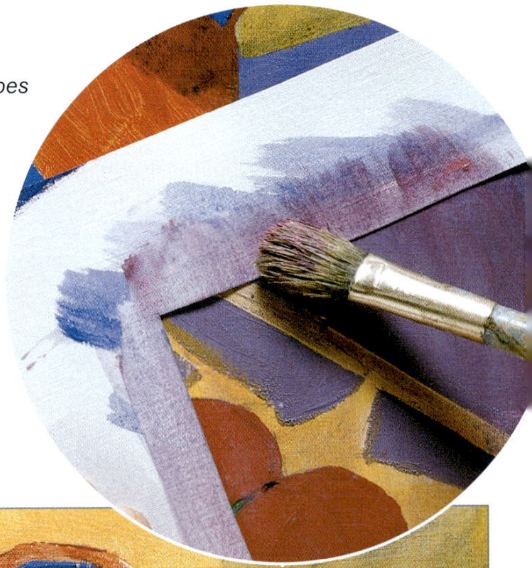

7

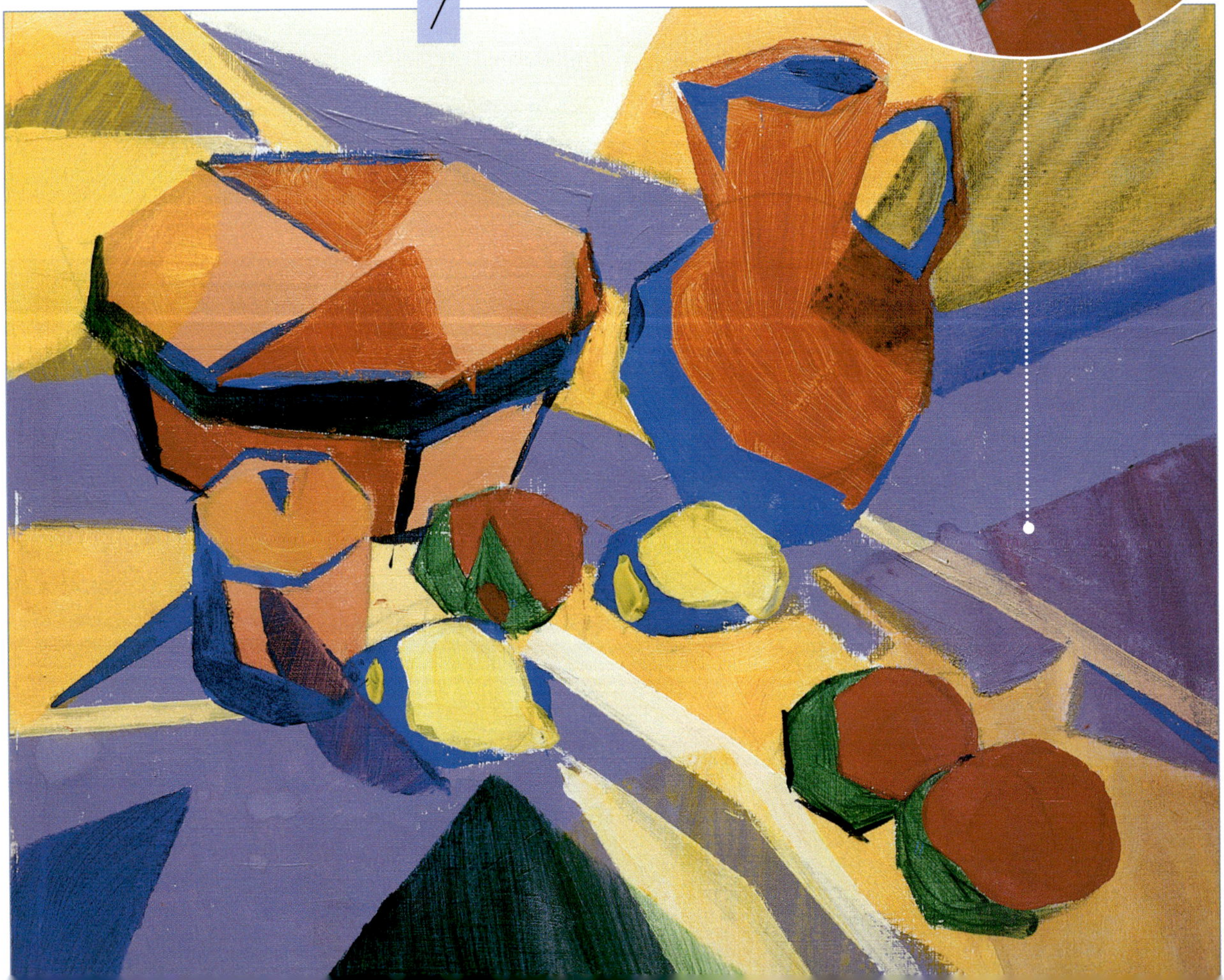

WAYS *of* APPLYING COLOUR

There are many ways of applying colour to the canvas. Each technique derives from a specific style and affects the final result of the painting; this means that, based on the method we choose, we can give it an impressionist, expressionist or stylized treatment. Here we review the most common ways of making the colours interact on the canvas.

If we wish to model cylindrical or spherical objects, gradation is one of the most appropriate methods for working with colours.

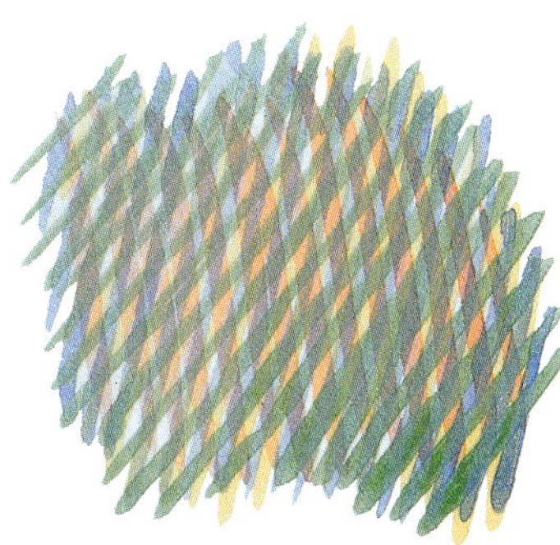

Hatch lines, so popular with pencils, can also be made with watercolours and gouache.

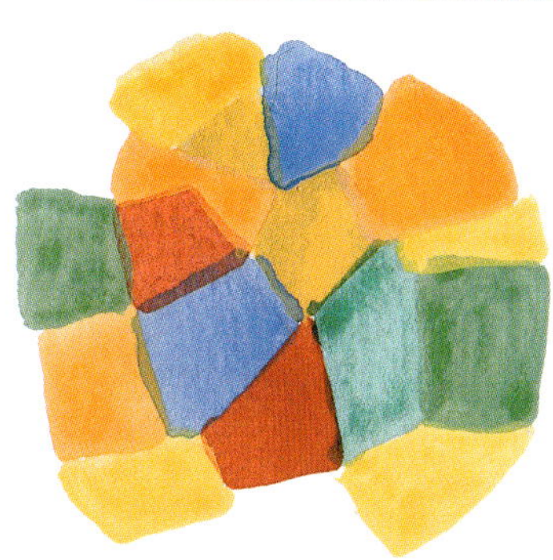

Working with blocks of colour allows us to insert different saturated colours whose contrasts cause the surface of the painting to vibrate.

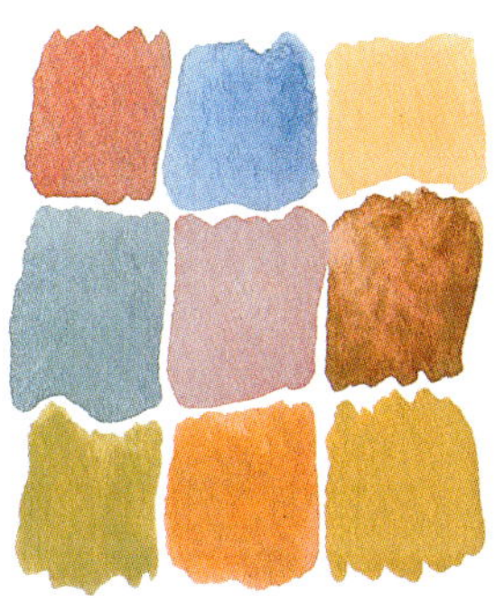

It is very common to work in blocks with watercolour, separated by a space that keeps the colours from optically mixing.

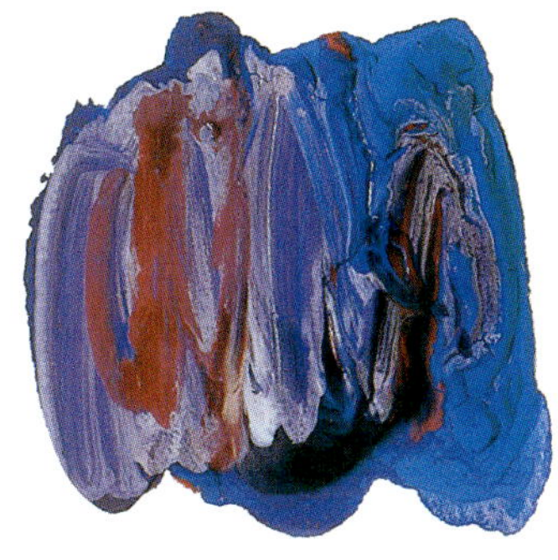

Impastos are created by working with dense and creamy colours mixed directly on the canvas. This may be the most expressive technique in painting.

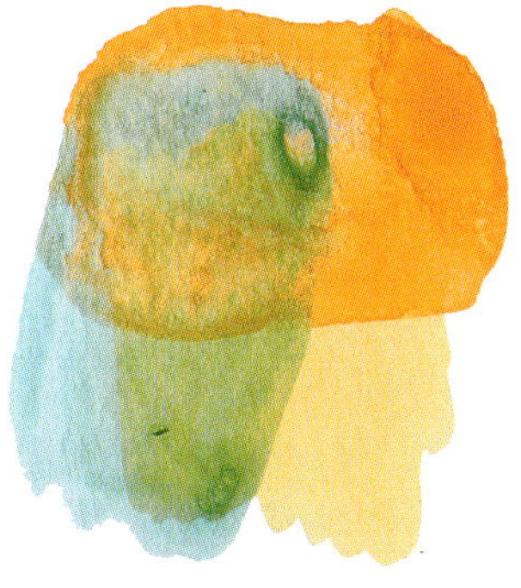

Glazing is overlaying light layers of colour that mix to form new colours. This technique produces very luminous paintings.

Washes allow colours to be mixed directly on the canvas; they can be used to create gradations and accidental mixtures of colours.

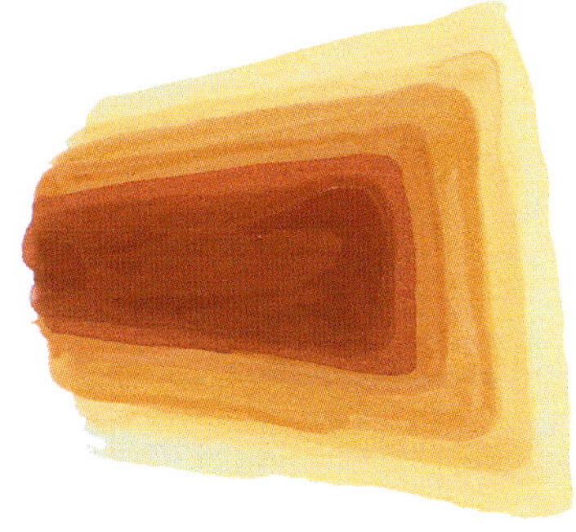

Here we overlay flat washes of colour that intensify or tint the underlying colours. A graduated effect can be achieved with tonal scales like this.

It is very common to work with strokes of uniform colour when using opaque paint like gouache, acrylic and oil.

High Key COLOURS

INTERIOR *with* *High Key* COLOURS

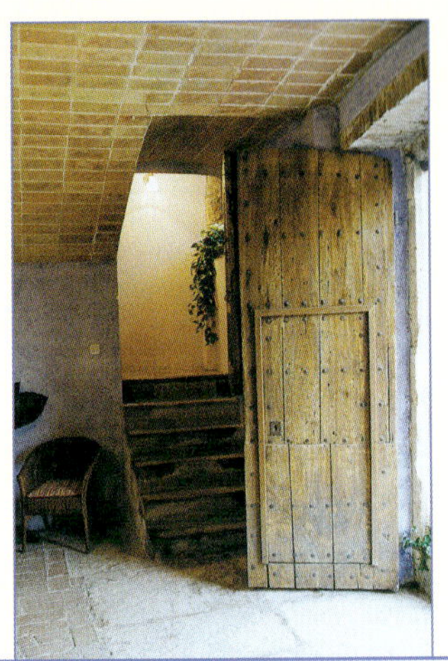

Saturated colour converts an everyday subject into an image with a much more striking personal style. The following example clearly shows this principle. To get the most out of the colours, we are going to forget about the more subtle shades and work with colours that are saturated and barely mixed. This is an enjoyable kind of painting and the technical process is within easy reach of a beginner.

We paint the canvas with an intense medium green acrylic that will dry quickly. Then we draw the interior with an oil pencil. The drawing is important, since the colours that we are going to apply will be flat and without modelling.

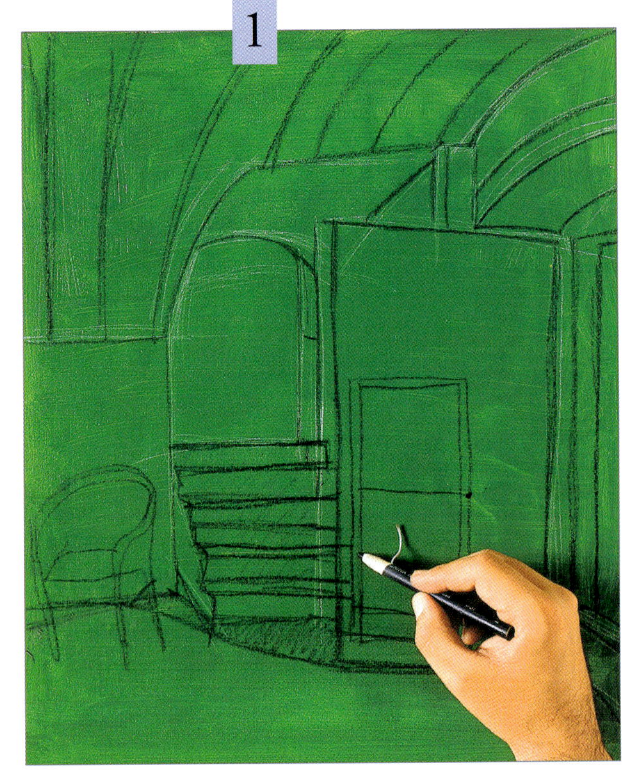

The background is painted with oils. Using cadmium red, cadmium yellow and white, we apply four juxtaposed flat colours as a gradation on the door at the top of the stairs. Then we paint the arches in the ceiling with short brushstrokes of reddish colours.

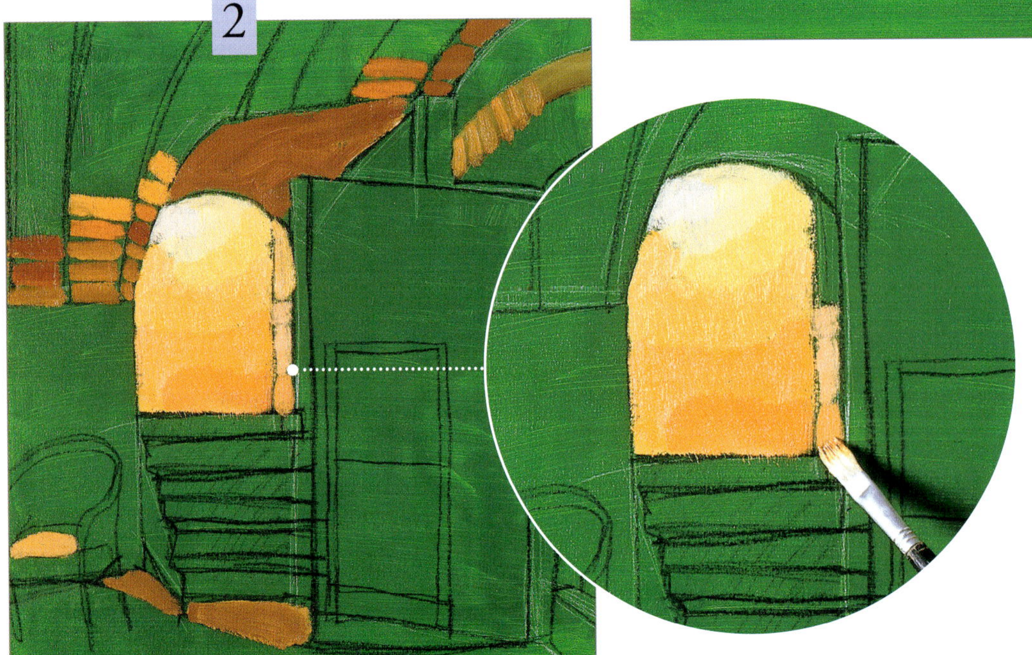

We recommend using a flat brush for working with thick and opaque paint.

Each illuminated area of the stairway must receive its share of flat orange colour. We cover the ceiling with brushstrokes that offer variations of ochre, yellow, orange, red and carmine. The green background stands out, acting as an outline around the individual bricks.

Now we colour the door. It is covered with vertical impasto stripes of colour, forming a light gradation. We begin with yellows, orange and red at the left, and sienna, ochre and olive green at the right. Some of these strips of colours are not completely flat, but contain a slight gradation.

3

4

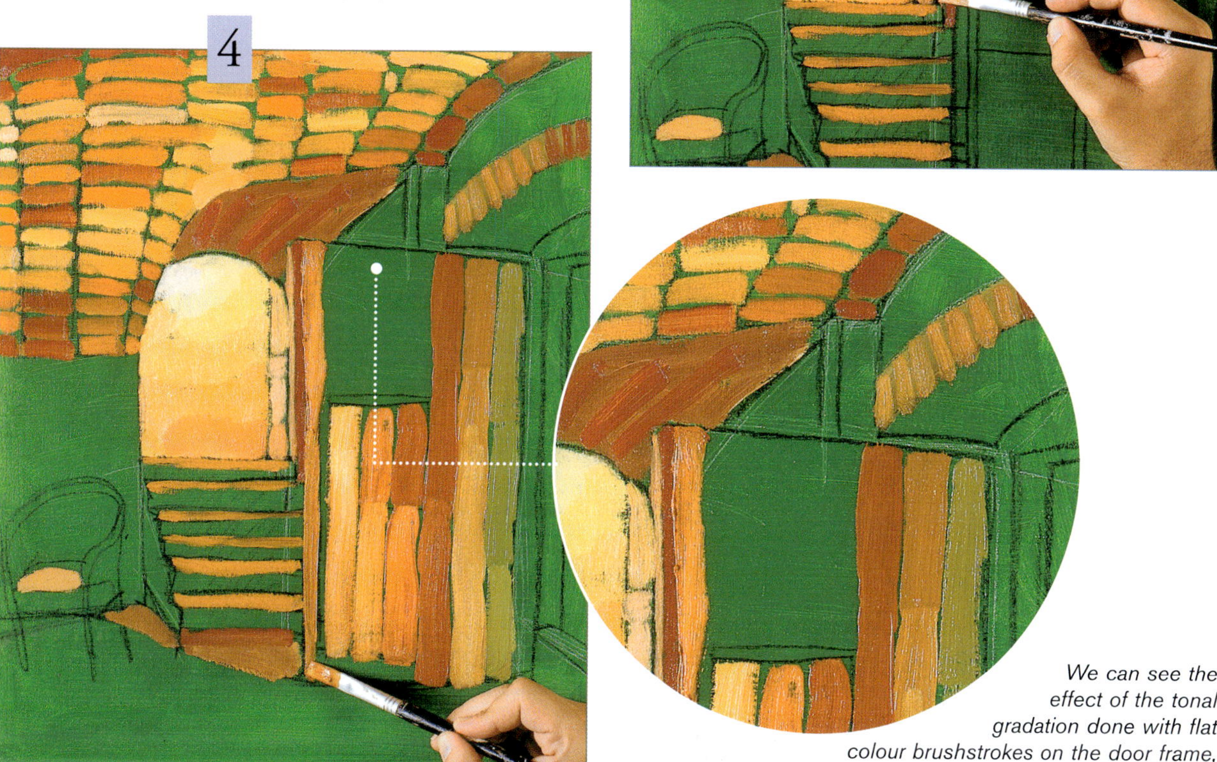

We can see the effect of the tonal gradation done with flat colour brushstrokes on the door frame, with the values going from light to dark.

5

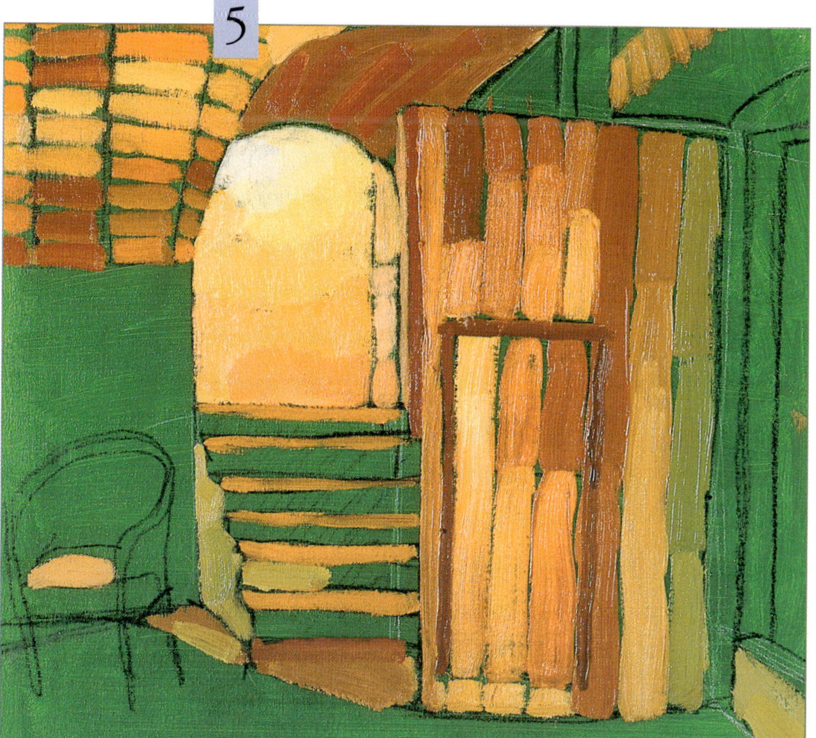

To finish the door, we cover the green background with wide new applications of reddish tones. Each brushstroke should differ from the colours next to it to correctly represent the row of wood planks that make the door. The moulding of the smaller rectangular door is painted with a smaller brush and carmine brown.

Tip

Sometimes it is good to make a sketch of the subject beforehand to analyze the placement of the colours, which will be warm in the illuminated areas and cool on the floor and the walls.

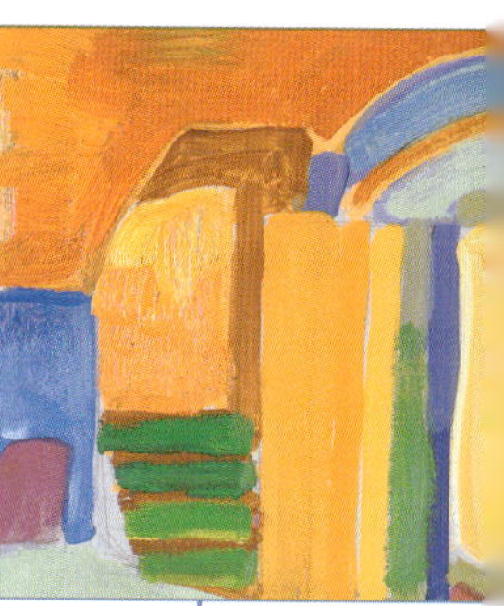

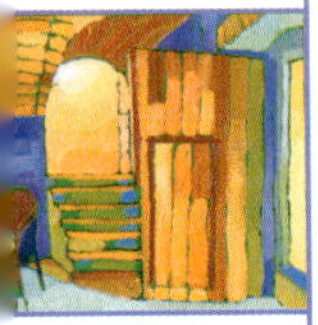

6

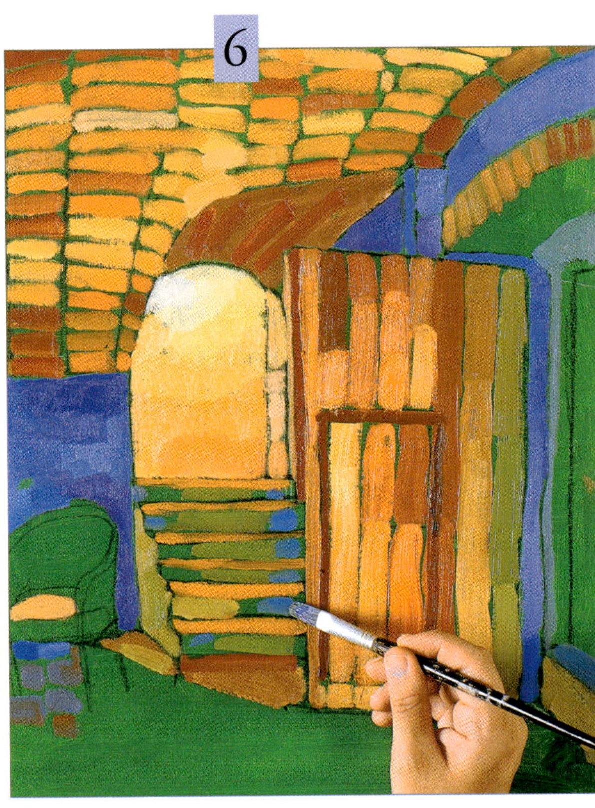

We paint the walls with blue colours. The bluish brushstrokes are unequal mixtures of cobalt blue, ultramarine and cyan. The latter is very useful for lightening the blues without causing them to lose saturation. Incorporating blue creates a visual effect between the warm colours and the cool colours, a strong contrast of complements.

Tip

A range of bright and saturated colours can be created with little mixing, little use of white and no black, browns or greys.

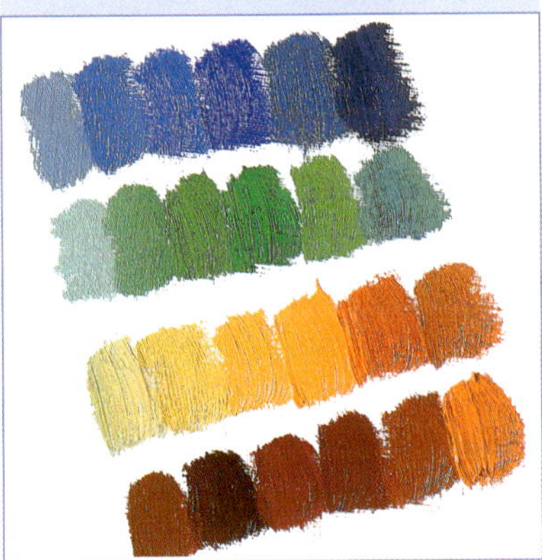

Finally, we apply the whitened green that covers the surface of the floor and the arched doorway, and the intense green of the steps in the stairway. The lines that we leave on the floor help indicate the texture and the perspective of the room. We paint the opening to the exterior with a graduated yellow.

7

While the bright saturated colours flatten the description of the space, the green lines that show through from the background direct the viewer's gaze to the interior of the painting and make the outline of each element stand out.

The chair, the only piece of furniture, is resolved with a few dabs of the colours red, violet and white.

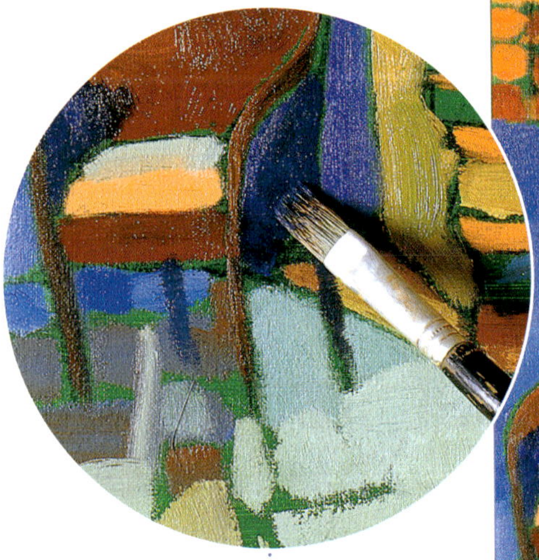

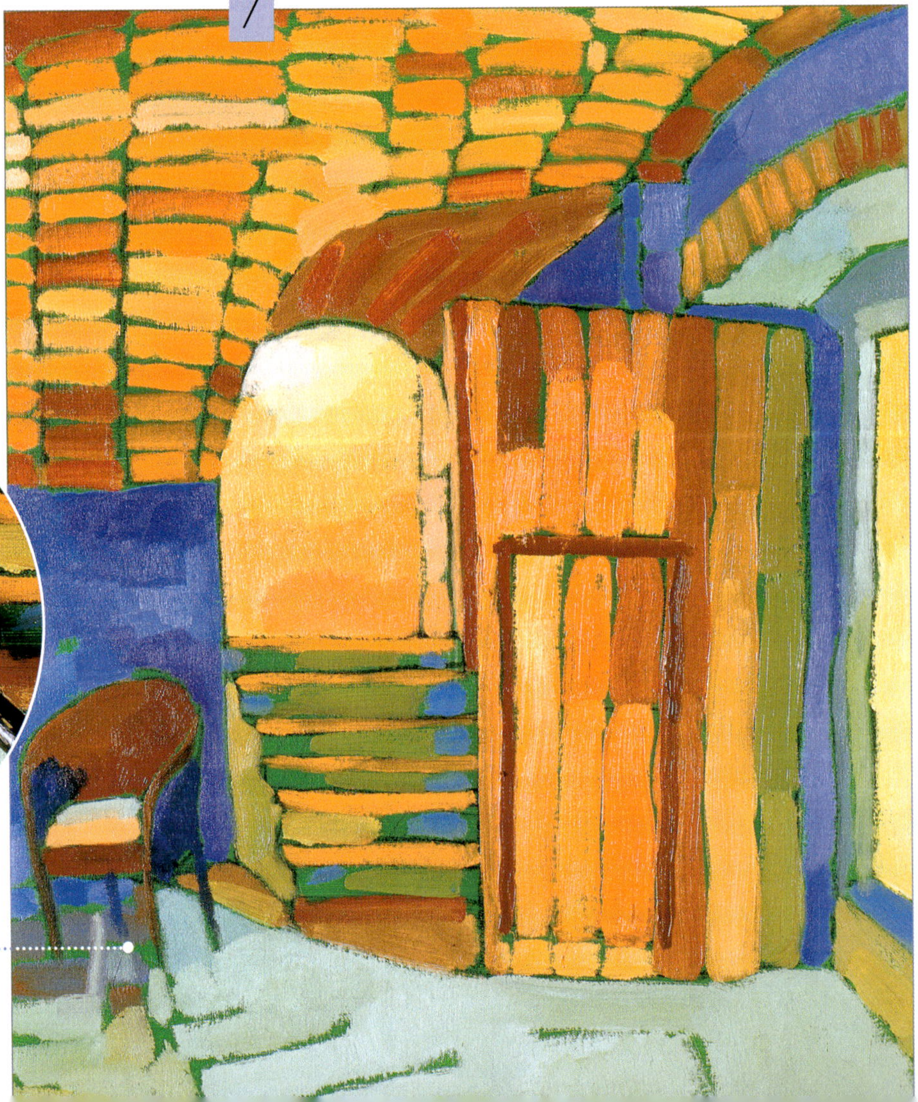

WAYS *to* SYNTHESIZE COLOUR

The exercise we have just presented constantly strives to synthesize the planes; the forms are constructed through the use of colour contrast instead of through modelling. Let's try to analyze, in an isolated and synthetic manner (without excessively manipulating the layer of paint), some techniques of applying oil paint to the canvas to better control the effect.

For the doorway above the well-lit stairs, we made a gradation by juxtaposing three areas of flat colour to form a small tonal scale.

To better learn how to create a tonal scale effect, we should practice with several colours. Here we have four values of green.

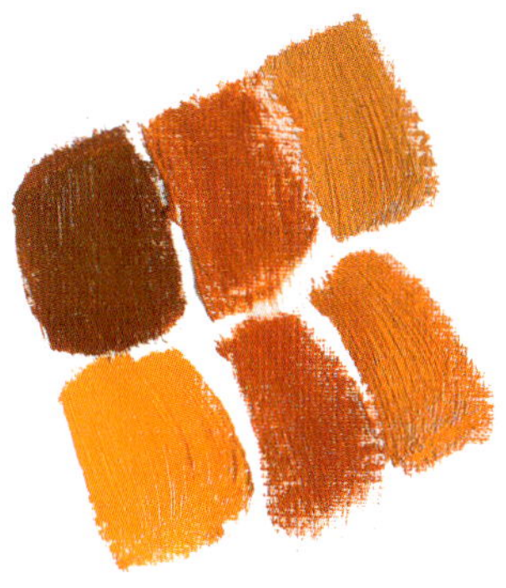

To paint the bricks in the arched ceiling, it is a good idea to develop various red colours. The two blocks of colour in the middle are reds (cadmium and English). These colours can be used to create new ones if we add yellow to the initial red in different proportions and/or a touch of white.

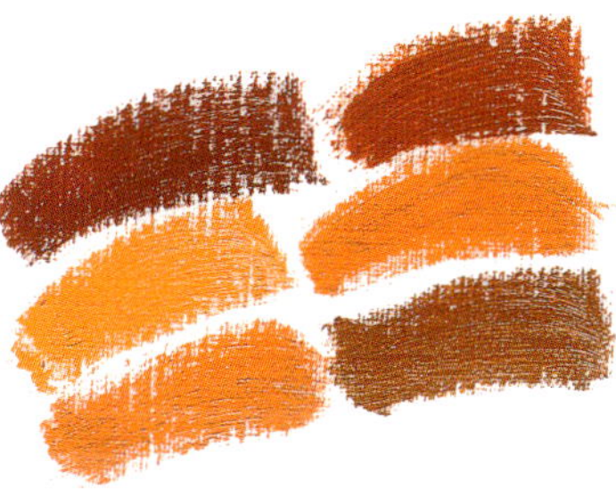

According to the consistency of the colour, we can make a series of bricks with more or less defined edges. If the paint is thick and not very diluted, the brushstroke will have a rough, broken edge.

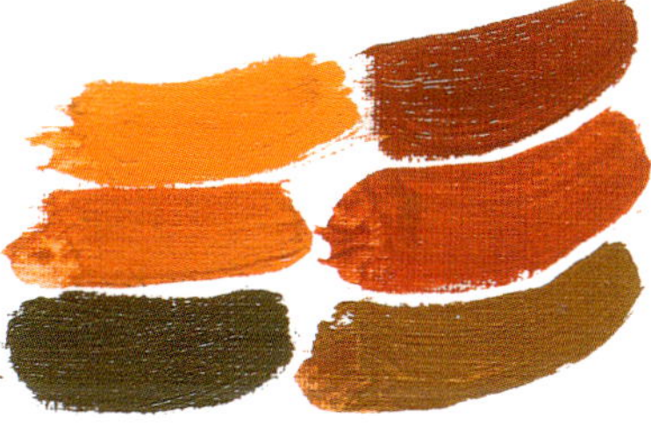

If, on the other hand, the colour on the brush is more diluted, the stroke will have a clean, straight edge. However, the dilution can cause the colour to be more transparent than in the previous case.

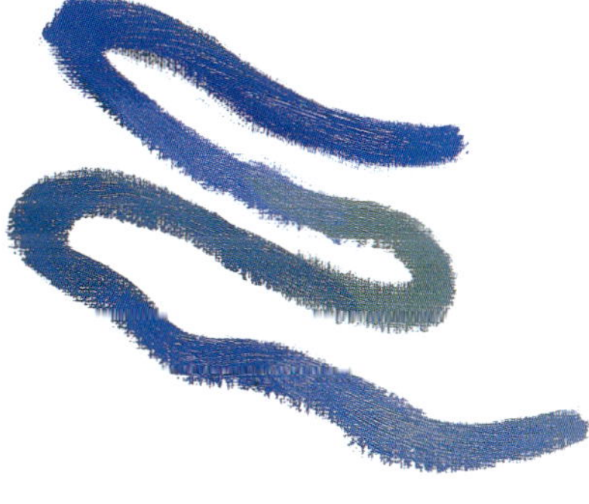

It is also good to control the gradation in uncommon situations. Here is a line painted with different blues that we have slightly graduated. They can simply be applied one next to the other and then lightly brushed where they touch.

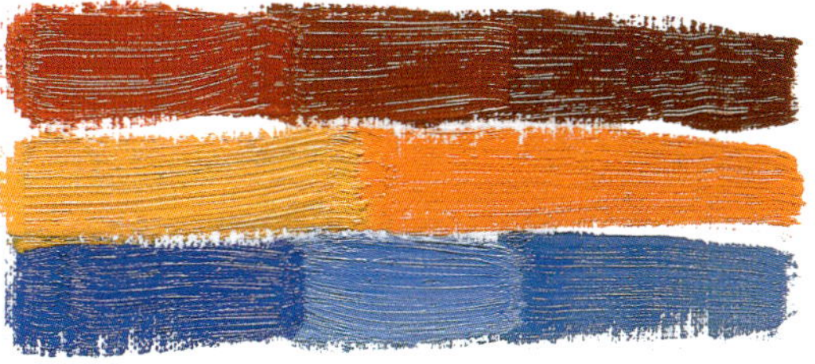

We painted the door using very dense and thick colours, one after another in a band. In the individual bands, there are no great variations of tone that would affect the feeling of continuity, but the adjacent bands do contrast with each other.

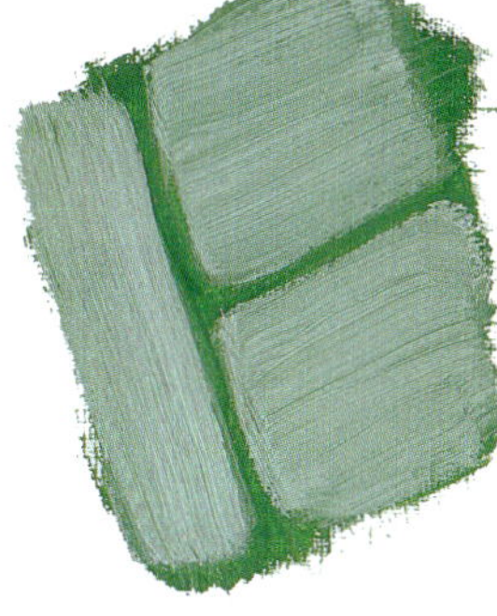

We work with areas of colour rather than lines; here they are applied to allow the background colour show through. These intentional linear marks complement the colours of the painting.

MONOCHROME

MULTICOLOUR *and* MONOCHROME

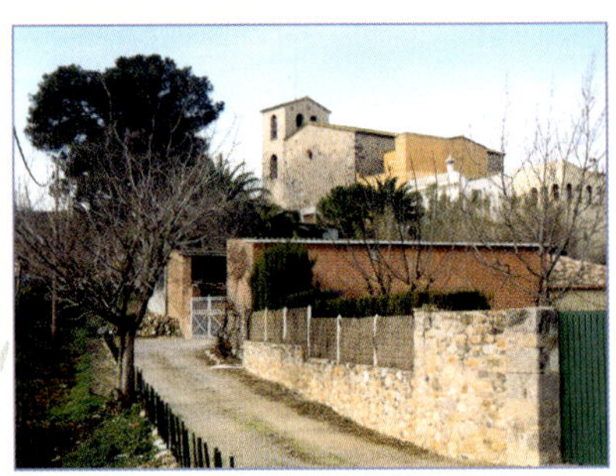

There are two clear ways of working with colour. One is working with many colours and the interaction of saturated colours, where each colour activates or is activated by adjacent colours that vividly contrast with them to create a vibrant and spectacular effect. The opposite case is the monochrome, which is created by making a painting from a single colour with variations in its tones and values. The result is more homogeneous, calming and harmonious. In the following exercise, we contrast these two ways of working, using the same subject. The medium we use is acrylic paint.

1

The initial sketch is extremely stylized. Using a graphite pencil, we first lay in the diagonals of the street and then we construct the main buildings as if they were blocks. When the drawing is finished, we go over it with a fine round brush and ultramarine blue paint.

The background is represented with gradations of cool colours, while the buildings and areas that we wish to emphasize are resolved with gradations of bright warm colours.

2

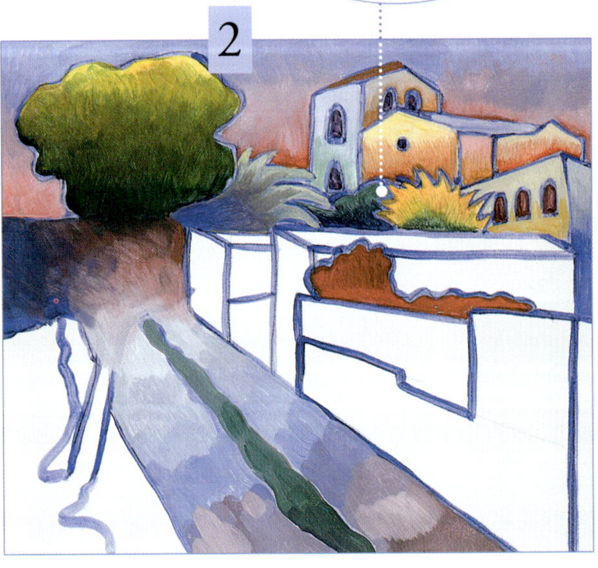

First we cover the largest areas of the painting with gradations: the sky, the vegetation and the road. We work with cool colours; blues modified with violet or carmine and yellows modified with green. The buildings receive a warmer treatment since they are the main focal point.

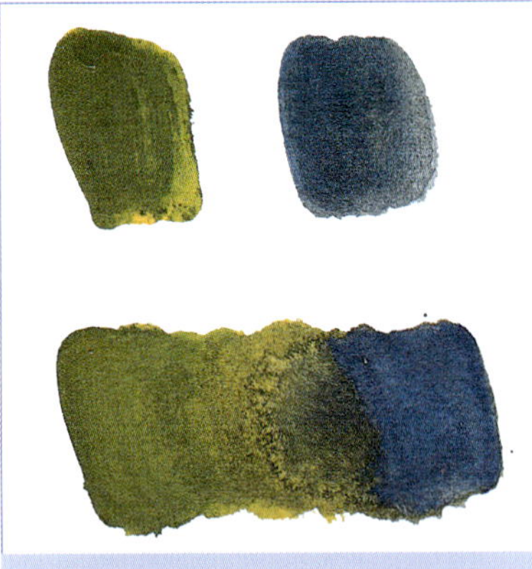

Tip

To work with gradations, it is necessary to learn how to intensify and tone down a colour. To do this, you merely place two saturated colours near each other and spread them with a brush until the space between them is covered with a gradation.

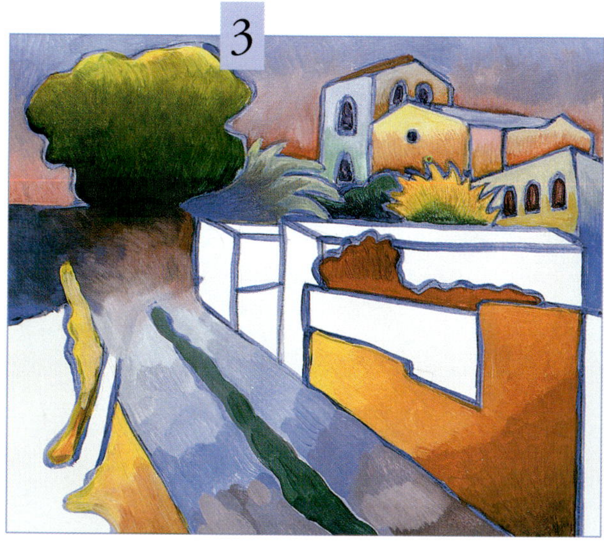

We are striving for a multicoloured effect. First we consider which areas we are going to paint with the brightest and warmest colours. Then we keep in mind that the adjoining areas should be covered with gradations of cool colour ranges so that the warm colours will stand out.

4

We can see how the illuminated walls, painted with gradations that go from yellow to red, are located between shaded façades painted with greenish gradations. We work on each area of colour by itself; this way, we preserve the initial blue line to achieve harmony and also maintain the importance of the line over the colour throughout the exercise.

Tip

When placing several gradations of the same range together, it is important that the same colours do not coincide. For example, a light yellow should be next to a red because two adjacent yellows will barely contrast with each other.

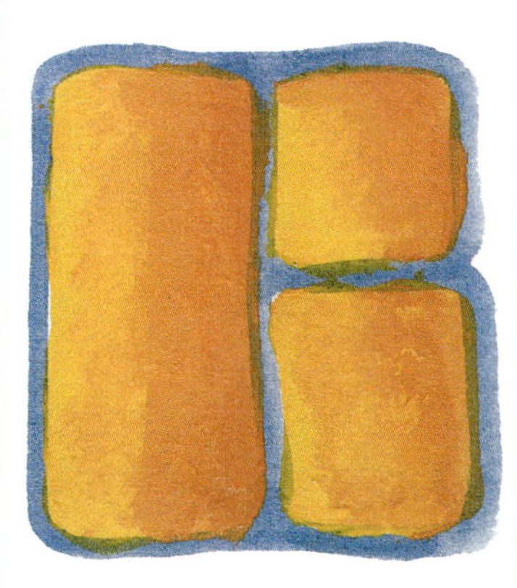

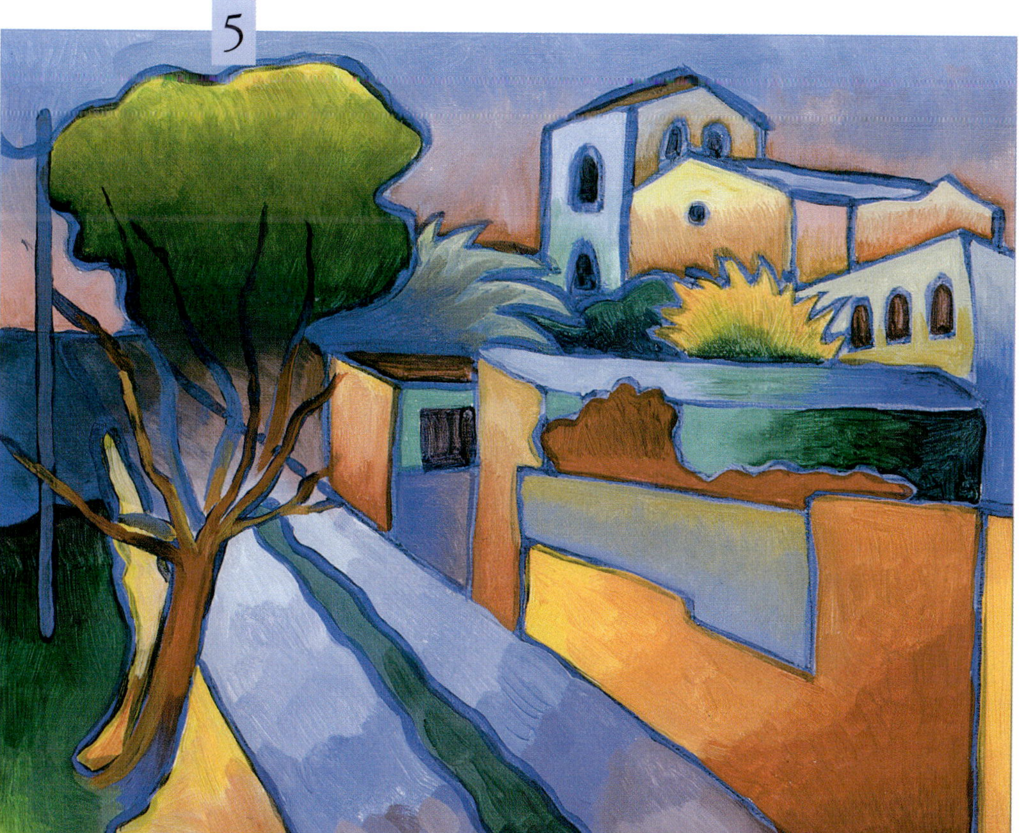

Working with gradations gives the painting a very volumetric effect. Despite the fact that the placement of the light is a bit disconcerting, this segmentation of colour enhances the final multicoloured effect, which is finished by painting the tree in the foreground and redrawing the blue lines that were lost during the applications of colour gradations.

Now we will carry out an exercise with a clearly monochromatic tendency. We will paint the same subject, but with a range of violet tones that go from magenta to ultramarine blue. Beginning with a pencil sketch, we rapidly cover it with a whitish violet in the sky and another bluish violet to create a gradation along the side of the road.

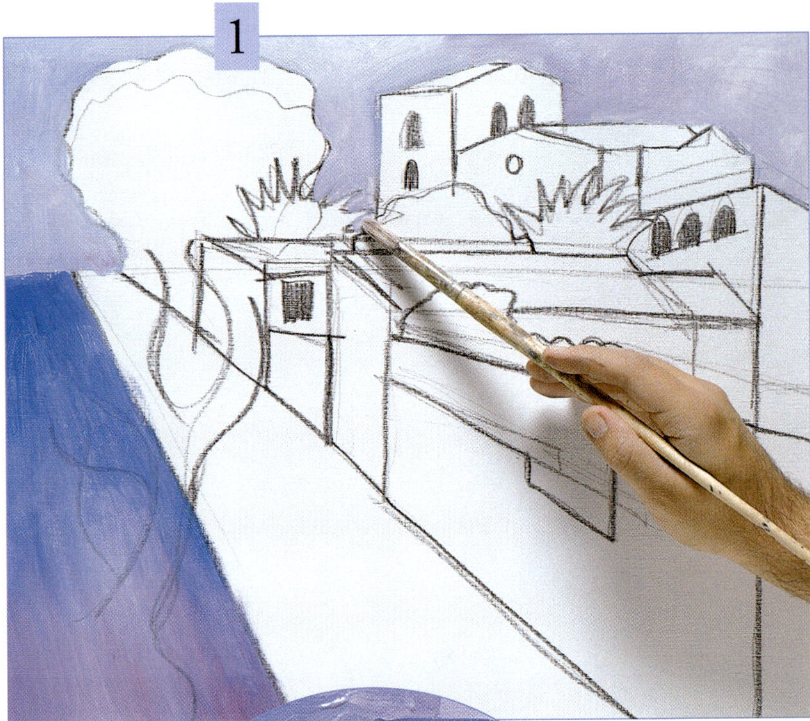

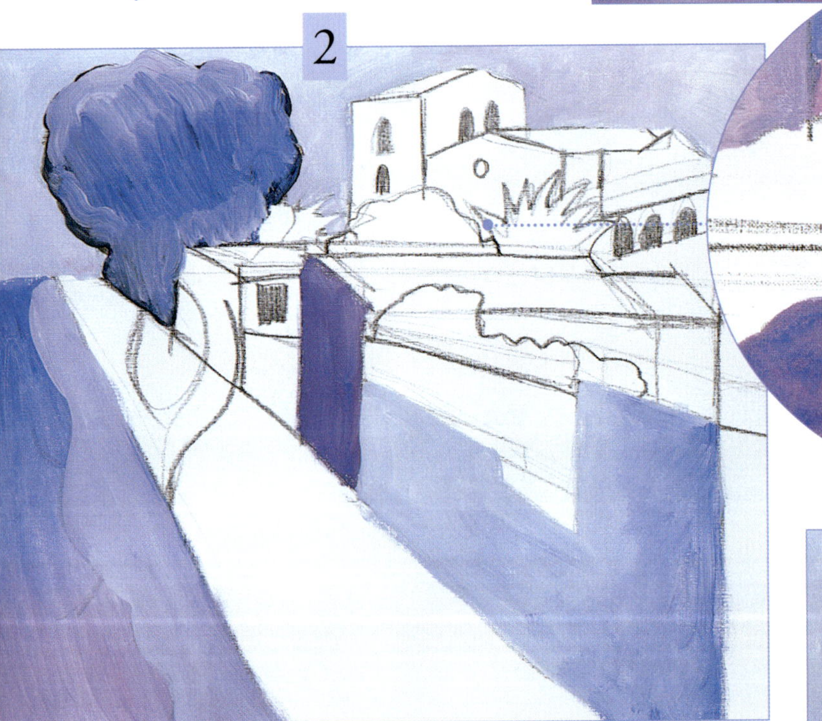

To create a gradation, we simply have to apply a layer of paint on the paper, in this case a magenta for the façade. While it is still damp, we add ultramarine blue to one side, blending it to create a gradation that goes to violet on the other side.

Using white, we lighten the new applications of blue on the façades along the road. The tree in the background is painted with darker paint; we mix it straight on the canvas, taking advantage of the still wet paint.

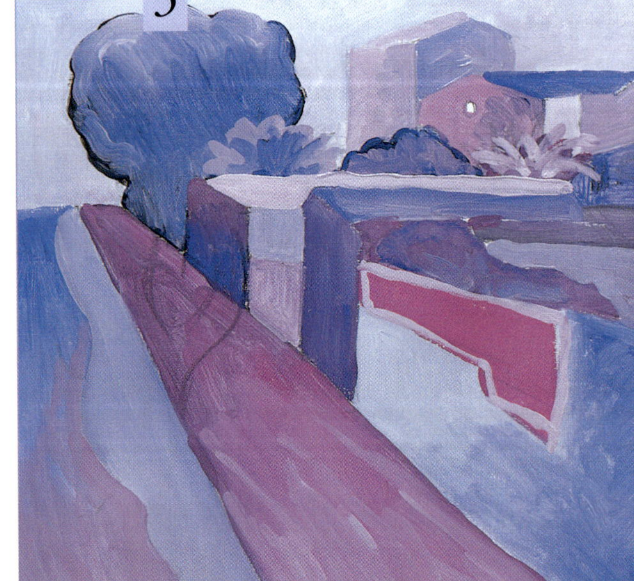

We cover the white areas of the paper with variations of violet. We must make sure that the adjoining colours have a different tone or value so that each area can be clearly distinguished, with each plane standing out through the colour contrast.

Tip

This exercise should be based on working on the large areas of colour that are outlined in pencil, without spending time on textures and unnecessary details.

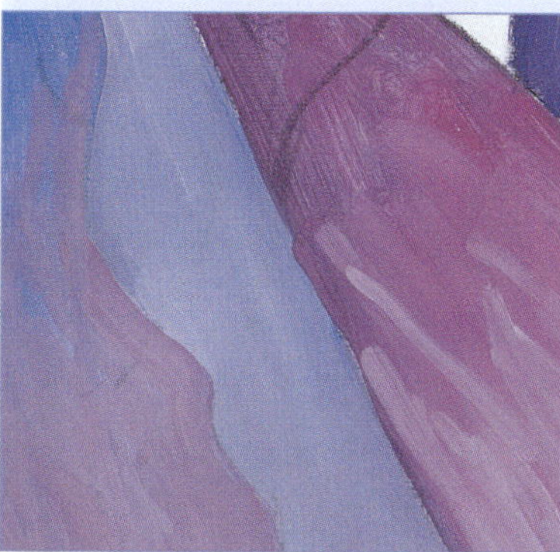

The entire surface is composed of violet areas that fit together like a puzzle. Using a fine round brush, we paint the lines that allow us to emphasize some edges that have become a bit blurred because of the similarity of the adjacent colours. We also paint the openings in the buildings with an intense violet.

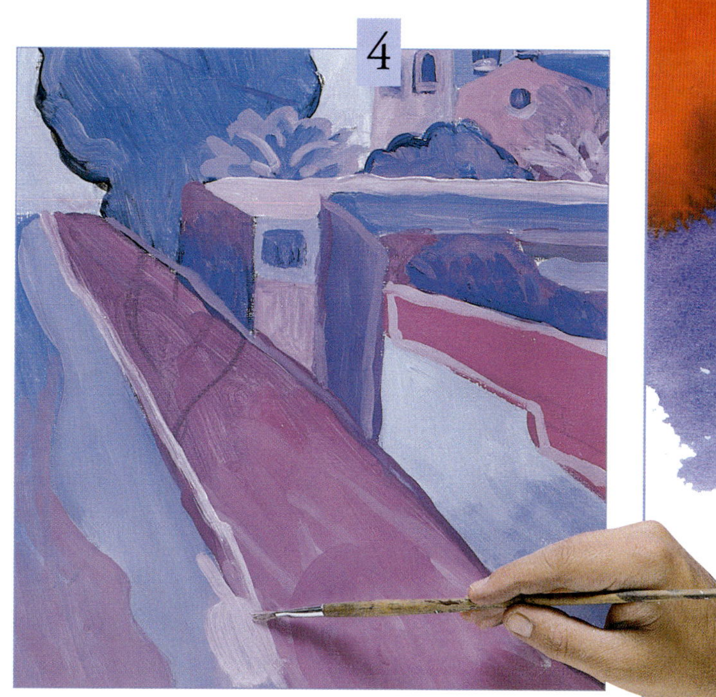

5

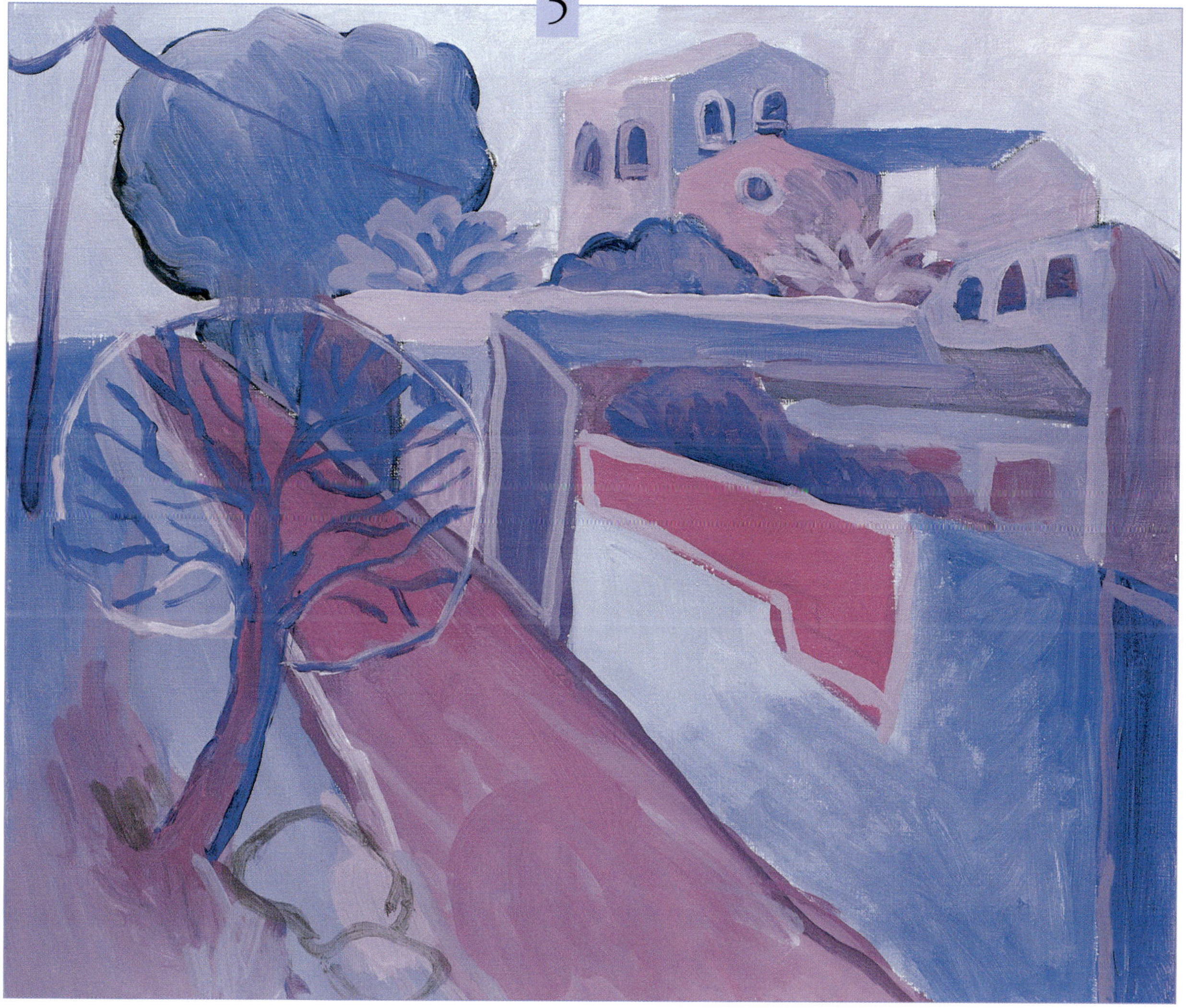

We conclude this exercise by extending a few more lines to modify the edges of some areas and by resolving the tree in the foreground. We do this by making a linear sketch with ultramarine blue. Then we fill in the trunk with violet and outline the branches with a whitish halo that gives it a more decorative feeling.

The PORTRAIT EXPERIENCE

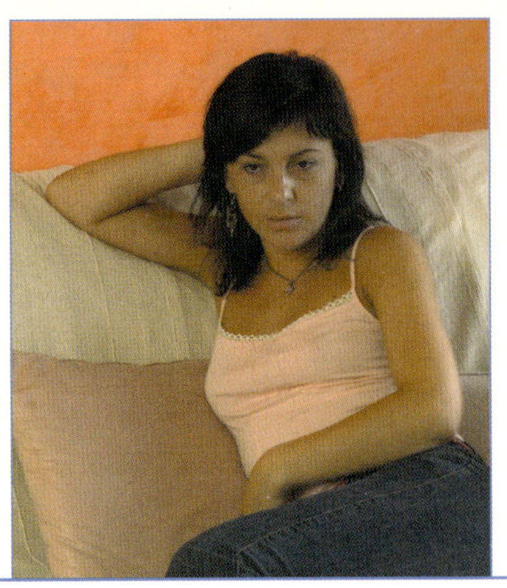

In the following portrait, we use acrylic paint as the medium. We will avoid a too realistic treatment, focusing on correctly representing the forms and paying more attention to colour. The main objective is the colour treatment of the flesh tones of the model, which will take precedence over the initial drawing.

1

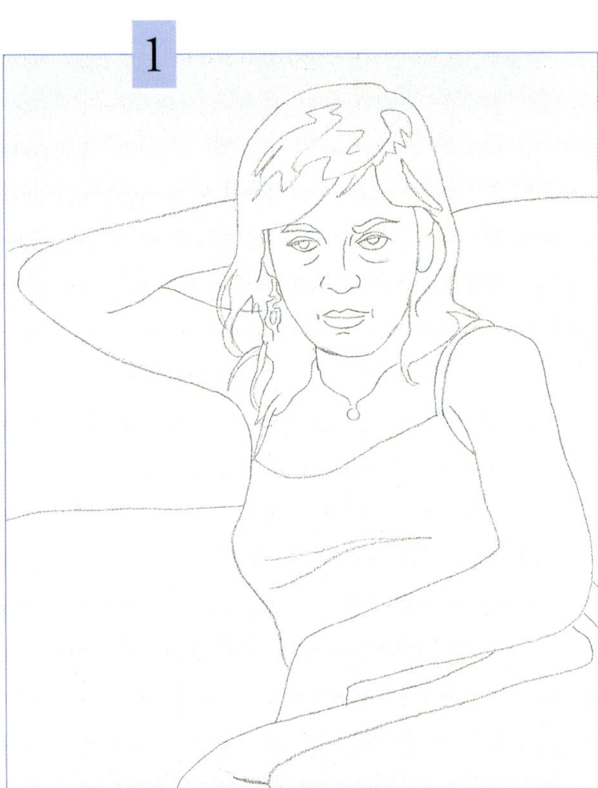

If we have experience, we can draw the portrait from a live model. If not, we can use a pencil to make a tracing from a photograph or project a slide onto a white wall. An outline is sufficient for use as a preliminary drawing.

2

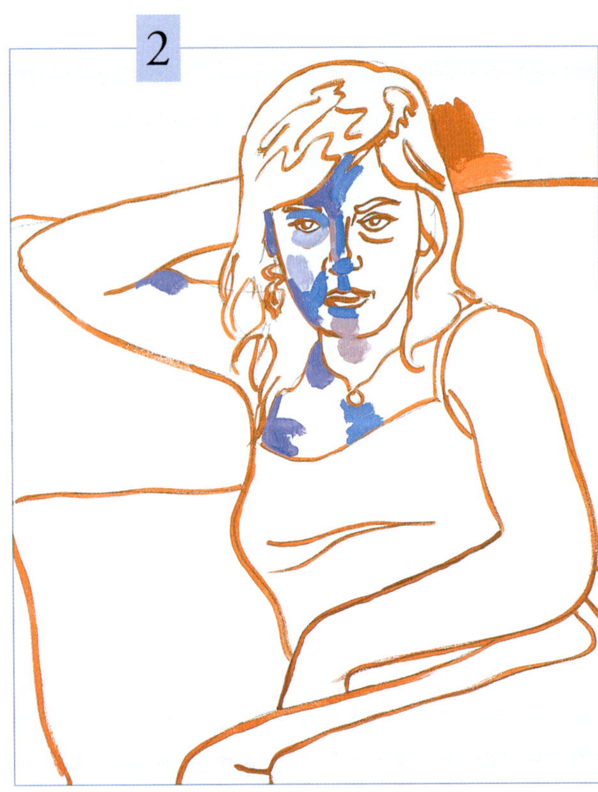

Using a fine round brush and red acrylic paint, we outline all the forms of the model with clear wide lines. These lines can be used as guides during the entire painting process. The first blue and violet tones are applied to the left side of the face.

Tip

The shaded areas of the flesh tones are indicated with variations of blue and violet, made by mixing ultramarine blue with a little carmine, white, cyan and grey.

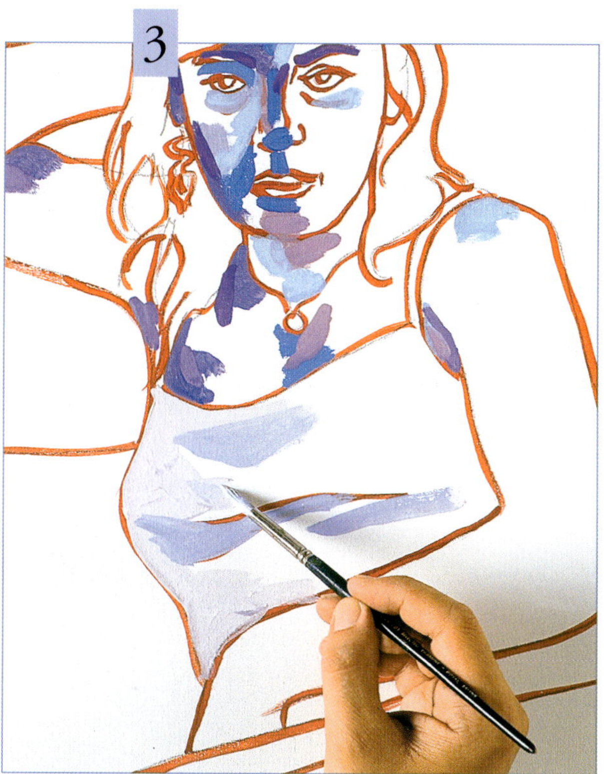

We paint the left side of the middle, the part we have decided to leave shaded, with cool colours. It is put together with blocks of colour as if it were a puzzle.

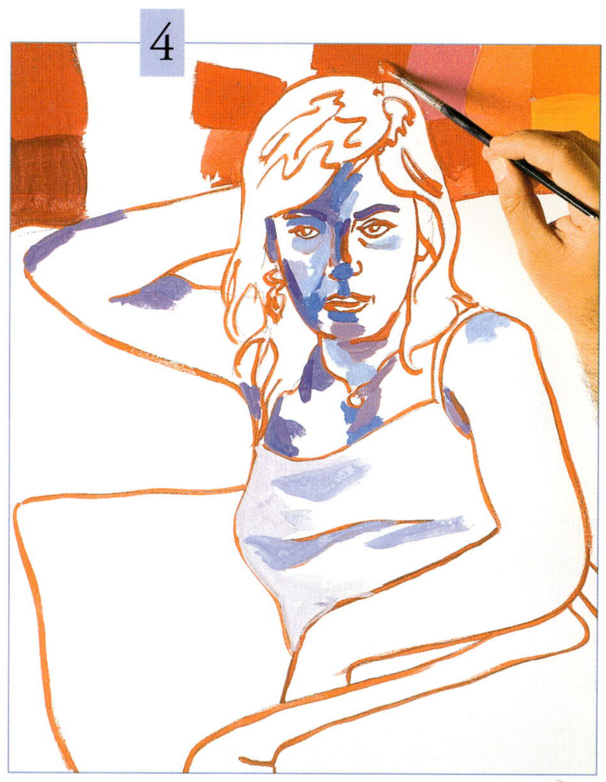

For a moment, we stop colouring the model to resolve the upper part of the background. The uniform magenta colour of the real wall is translated into a series of blocks of warm colours. We place yellows and oranges to the right and blocks of carmine tones to the left, simulating the natural flow of light.

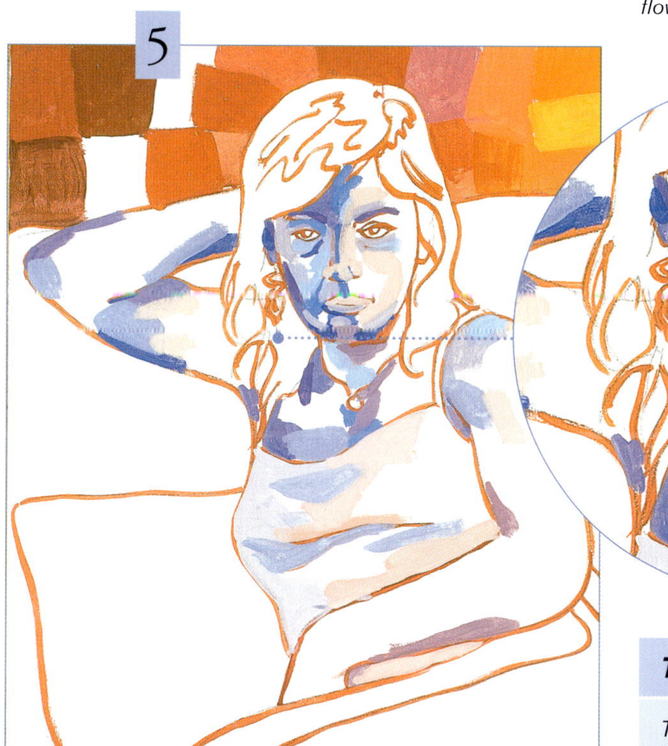

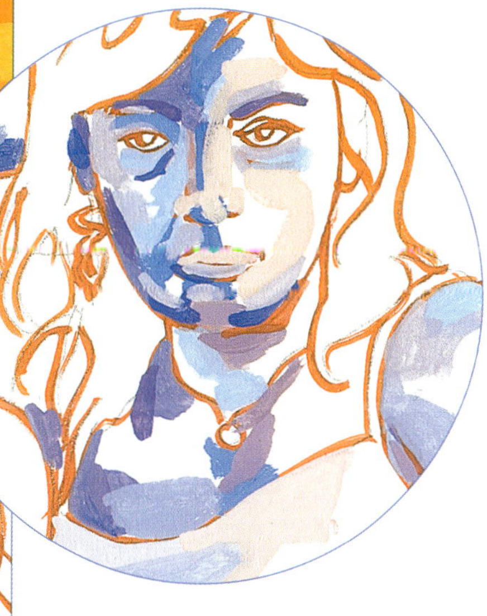

In an enlargement of the face we can see how the original red lines are not completely painted over. Some of them are quite visible and complement the different colours.

We approach the shaded area by juxtaposing bluish brushstrokes; the illuminated side, on the other hand, has pinks that are more reminiscent of the natural flesh tones. We try to model the face using these new applications of colour.

Tip

The background at the top of the painting is covered with squares of juxtaposed warm colours that break up the uniformity of the wall by adding a more attractive play of colours.

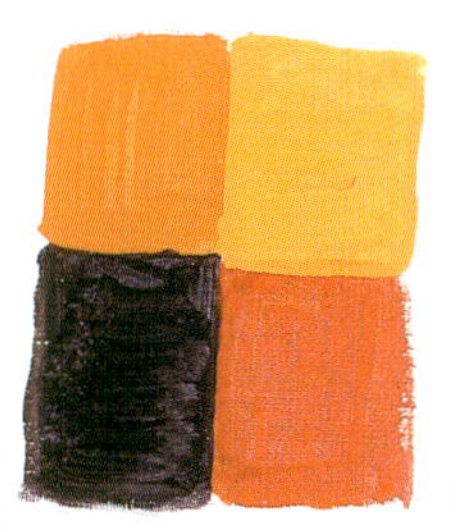

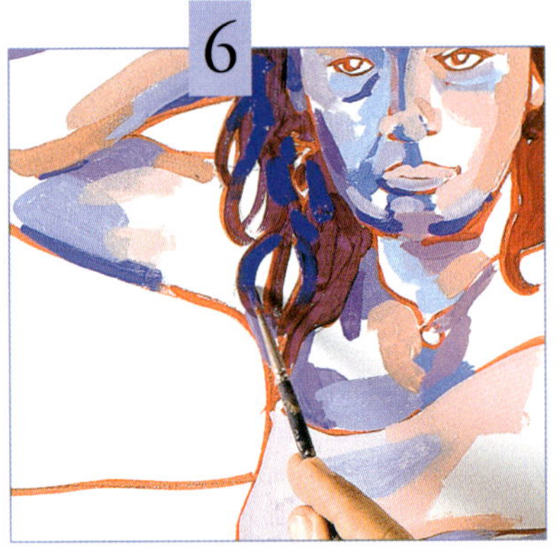

We use a sienna colour practically straight from the tube for the hair. When the sienna is dry, we apply orange paint to the right side of the hair and blue to the left to differentiate between the shaded and illuminated parts.

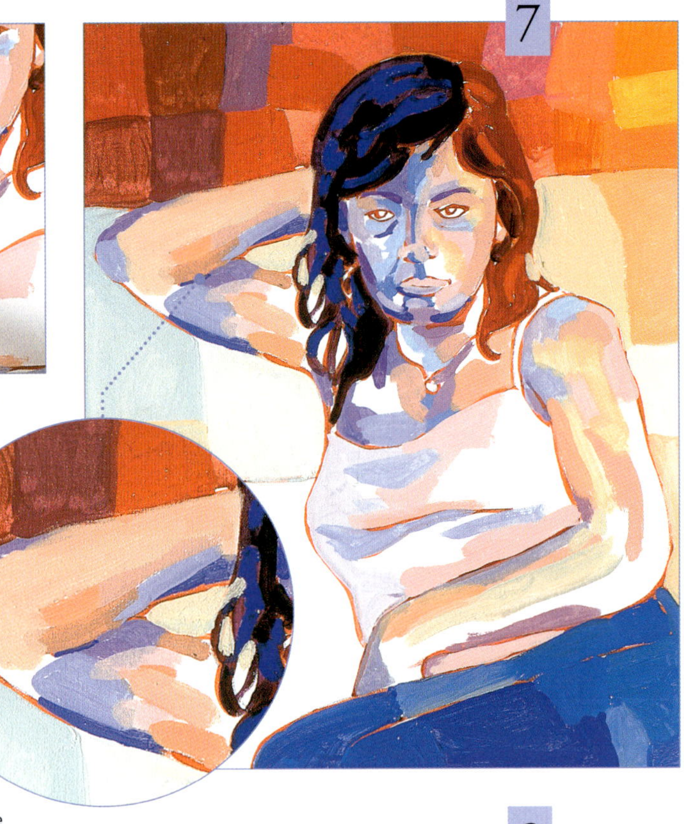

The sofa is painted with several squares of whitened colours. A well-designed background should keep the focus on the model, and the forms, the tones and the colours in it should be balanced and should complement the overall design. The pastel coloured squares add vertical and horizontal lines that reinforce the composition of the painting.

There are no rules that determine where each colour should go – the treatment is somewhat anarchic. Let yourself, then, be guided by intuition and take care that one colour does not clash with the one next to it.

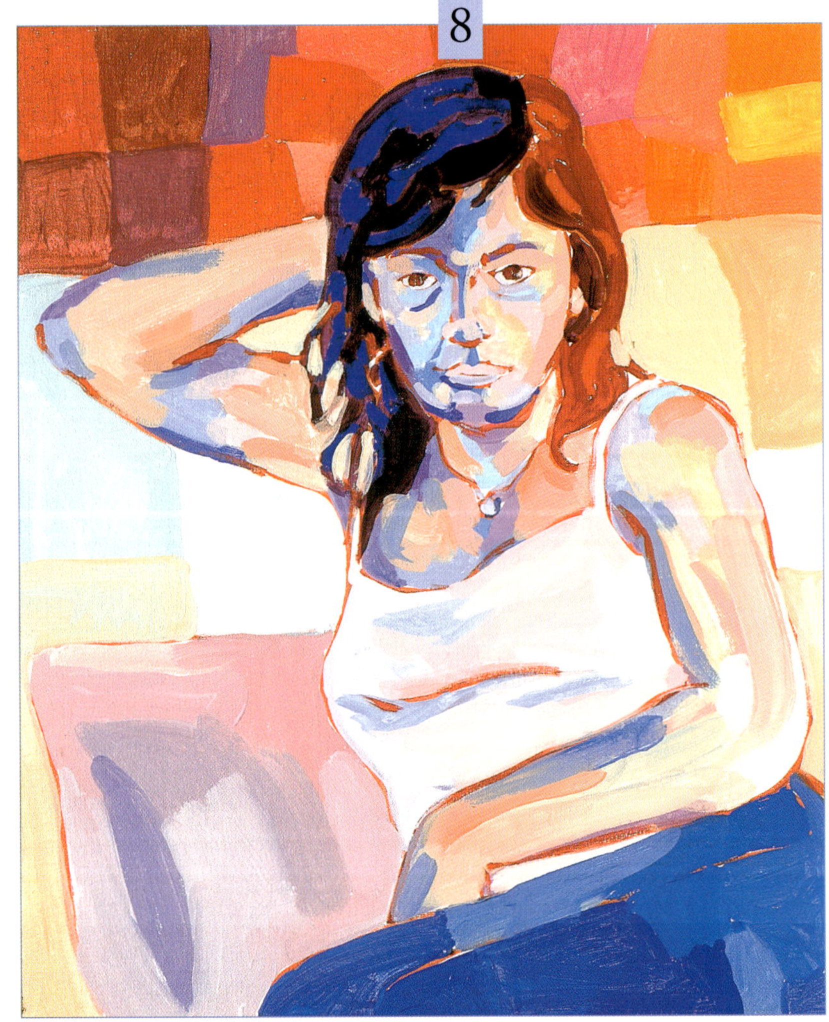

We finish modeling the figure with new applications of warm colours: pinks and light oranges for the skin tones and pinkish white on the shirt. The repetition of colours in several areas of the skin helps to preserve the unity of the painting.

Tip

We also paint the sofa with geometric patches of colour. The outline of the figure is reinforced by reducing the intensity of the colours, which are mixed with white, giving them a more pastel tone.

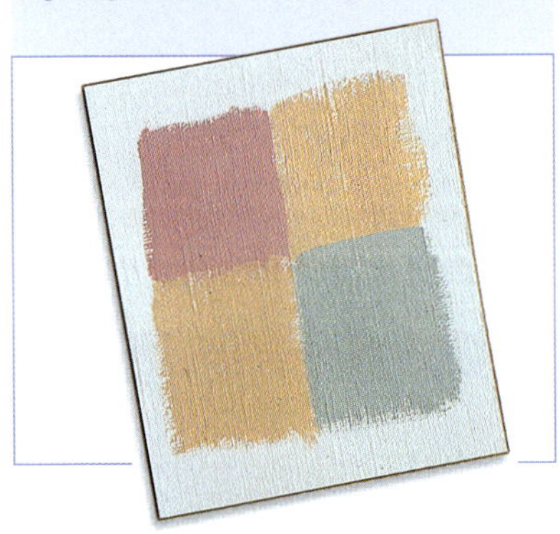

9

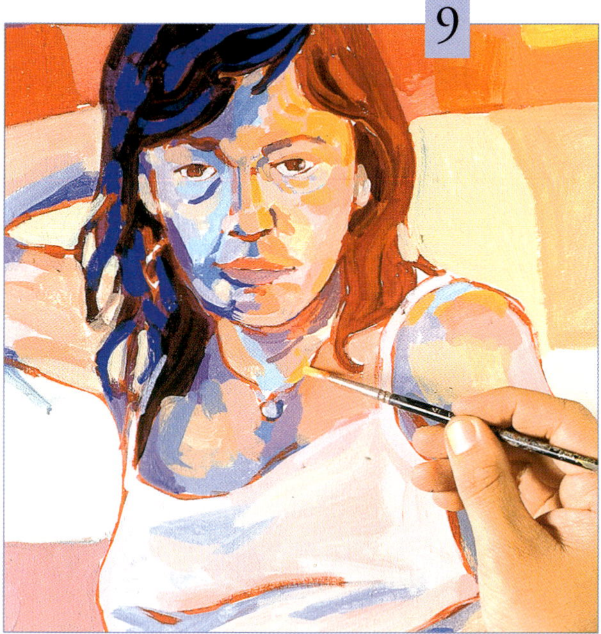

Using a fine round brush, we add orange and yellowish touches to the outline and the arm of the right side of the figure. We also add blue and violet to the outline and arm on the left. The contrast between warm and cool colours adds to the sense of volume and creates more contrast between the areas of light and shadow.

The final applications of colour should be very saturated, opaque and small. They should contrast and clearly be different from those applied in the earlier phases.

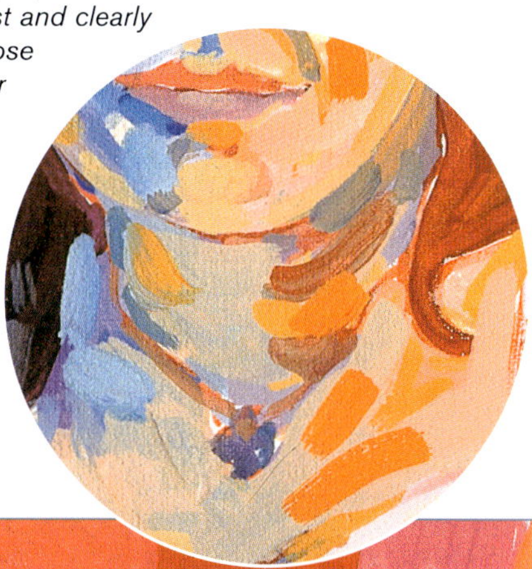

10

We make the final applications of blue, orange and yellow with more opaque paint to create an expressive effect. With the contrast between the warm and cool colours on both the face and the body and some very loose brushstrokes laid over the skin tones, we have created an unconventional portrait that is full of life.

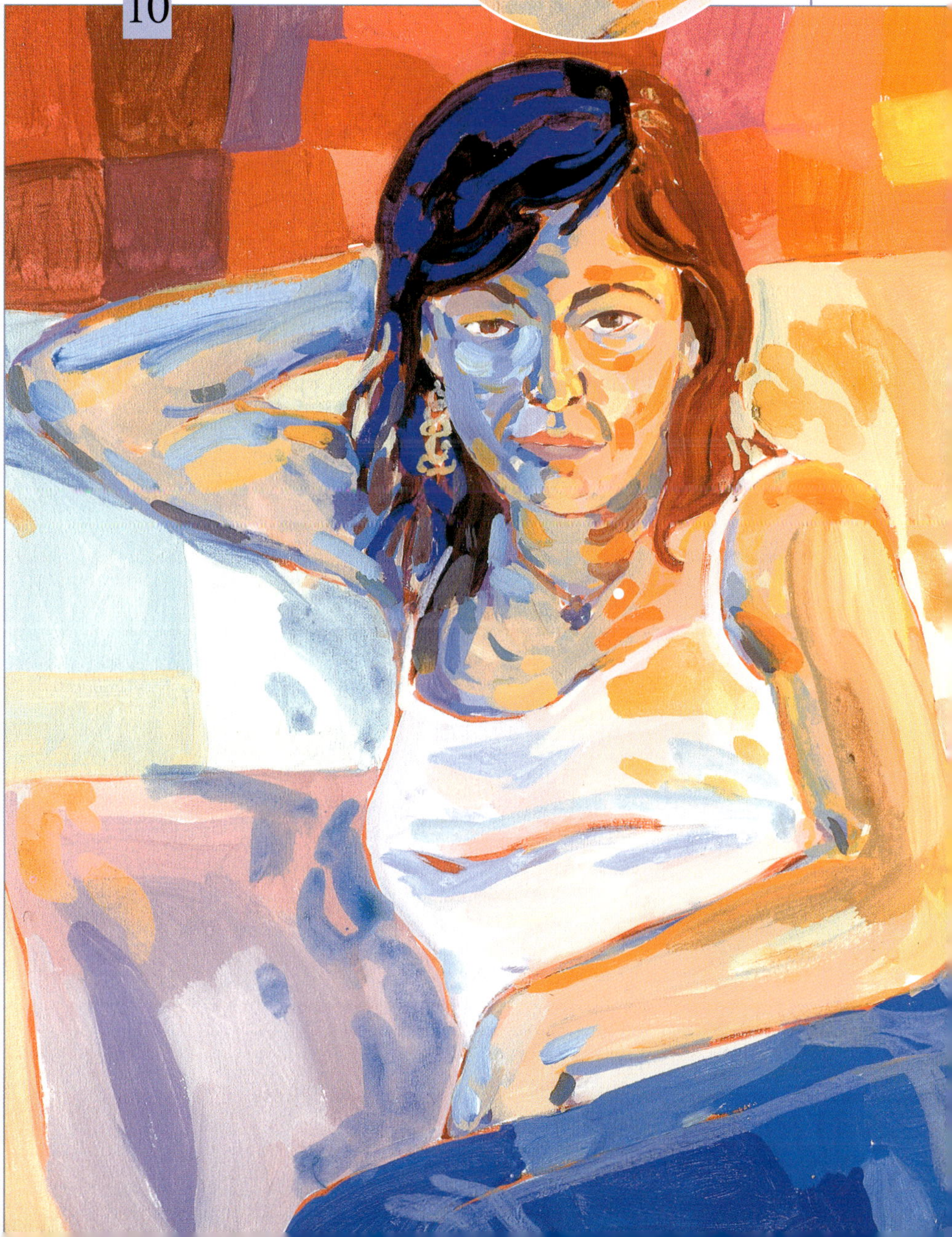

Tip

The background of the painting should be designed as if it were an abstract composition upon which the figure will be placed. Here is a sketch of the background colours.

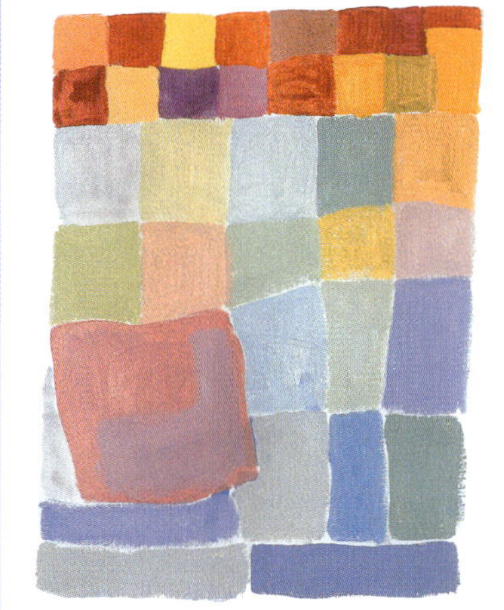

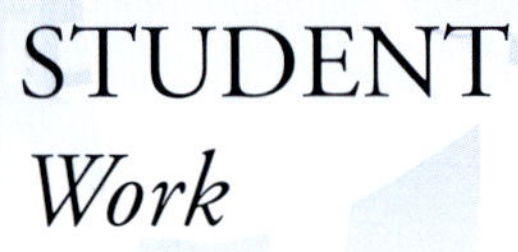

STUDENT *Work*

Now let's see how the previous exercise, done by a professional artist, was done by art students still in the learning process. The students, just like the artist, have painted portraits choosing different models and compositions in which the colour treatment becomes the main objective. Different ways of working and interpreting the subject offer diverse results, all equally interesting and noteworthy. Learning from their successes can help inspire you and help you make progress in your work.

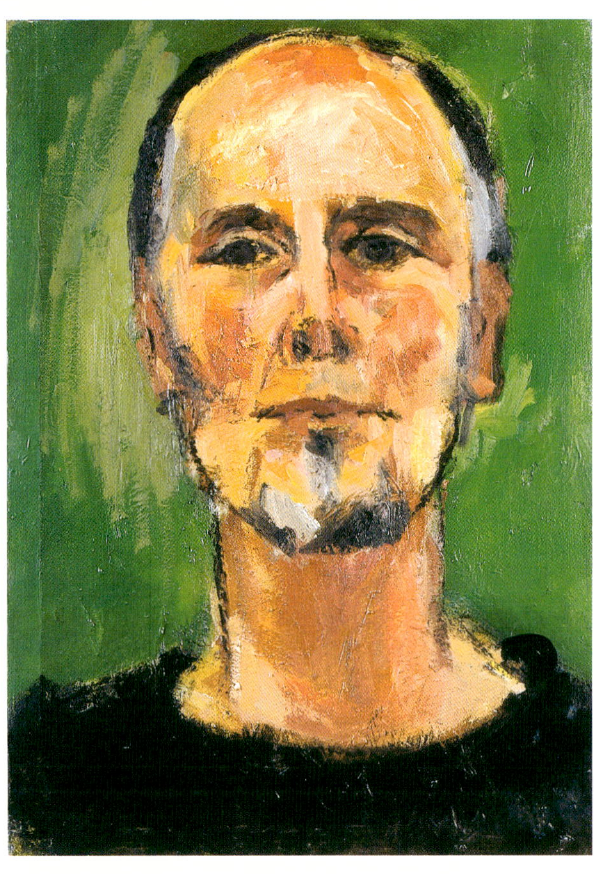

The student built up the skin tones of the face with pinks, ochre, sienna, yellow and other brown tones derived from an orange colour range. The background is painted with green, the complementary colour of orange, to add more relevance to this colour range and emphasize the outline of the figure. This contrast accentuates the strength of the colours in the face. Painted by Gabriel Sabanés.

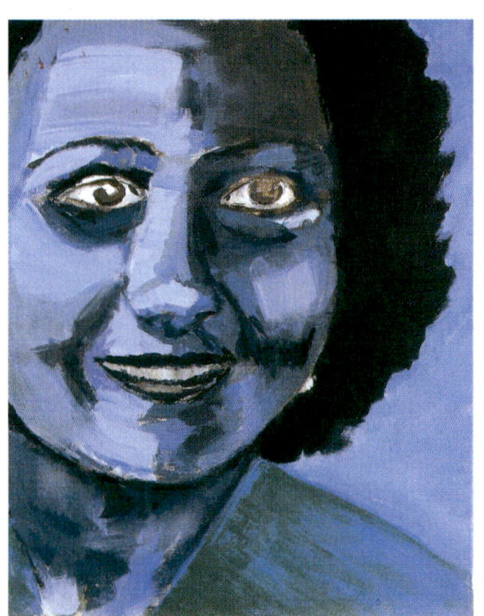

The skin colour was built up by overlaying blue colours, first working with very diluted colours and mixing ultramarine blue and cobalt blue with ochre, sienna and black. Next we can see the thicker light blue colour in the lightest parts of the face. The modeling is succinct and results in a very stylized treatment. Painted by Dulce María Rodríguez Martínez-Sierra.

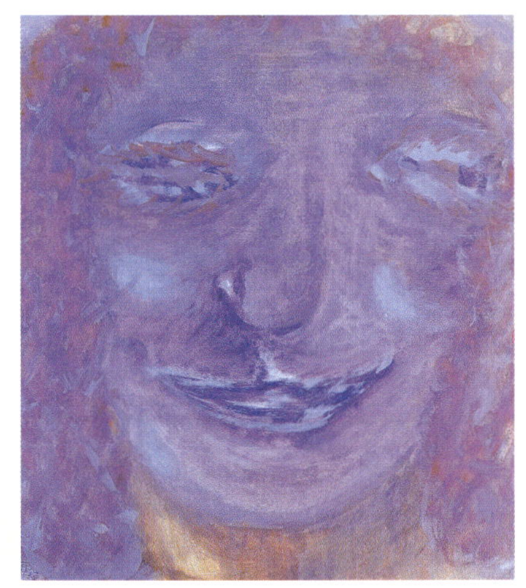

In this composition, the figure emerges from the overlaying of blended colours that barely define the hair and facial features. The absence of a preliminary drawing gives the work a very painterly look that is created with just four colours: magenta, violet, pink and a sky blue mixed with a lot of white. There is an intense distortion of the figure with blurry outlines, which is only identifiable through the moderate contrasts of the colours. Painted by Caterina Solivellas.

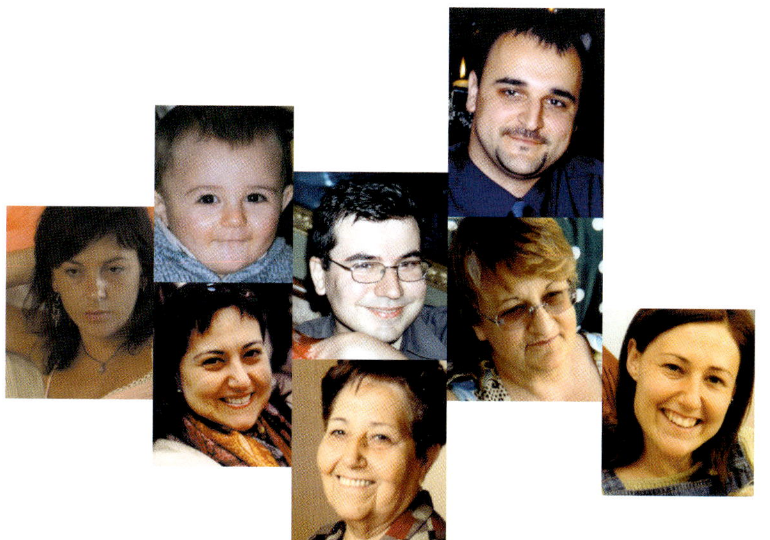

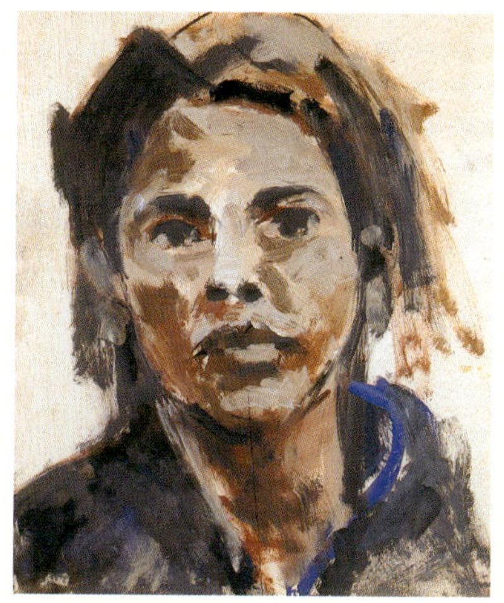

Here is a monochromatic treatment with sienna, white, black and a little ultramarine blue. The colour of the skin tones is created with values of sienna mixed with white and we can see the same brown colour mixed in different proportions with black in the hair, facial features and the large shadow on the neck. In the dark mixture in some parts of the hair and in the clothing, we can make out the presence of ultramarine blue, which slightly accentuates the monochromatic browns. Painted by Gabriel Sabanés.

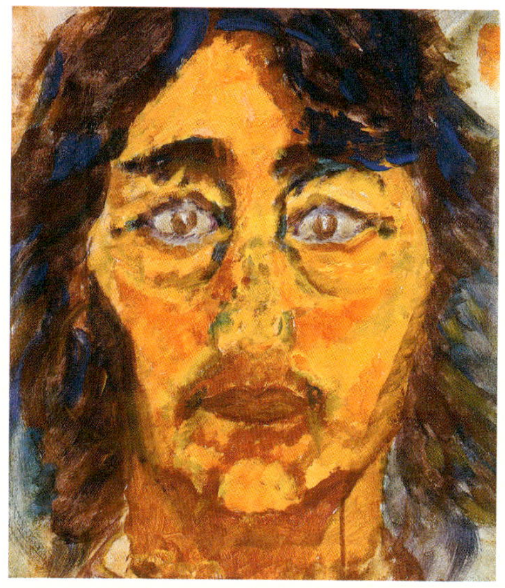

A drawing with a lack of academic criteria, the use of bright colours, and a brushstroke full of colours that are mixed directly on the canvas define the approach of this painting. The skin tones seem lively, built up with a range of roughly mixed warm colours. Touches of ultramarine blue revive the contrast of colour ranges in the dark parts of the hair. The only lines are in the eyes, which become the focal point of the work. Painted by Rosa Puigcercós.

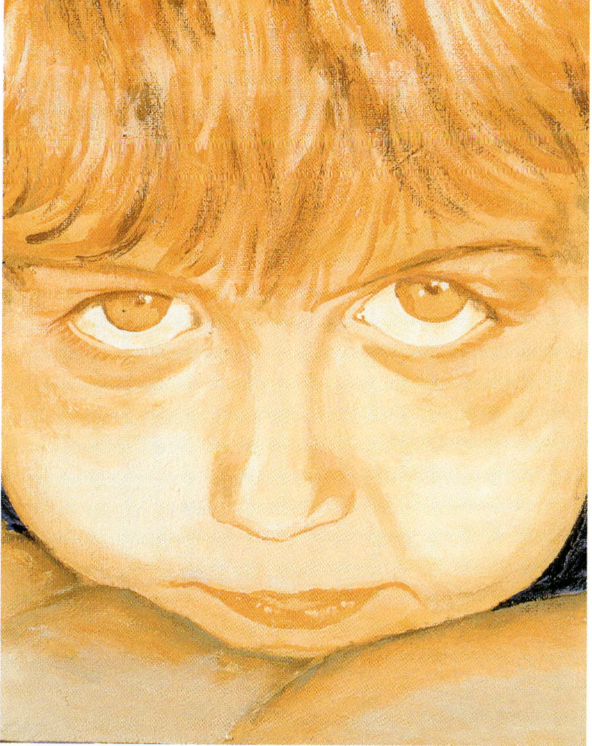

This other monochromatic treatment, painted with an orange-brown, barely shows changes in tone. The different chromatic variations were made by tinting the colour with white and darkening it lightly with a little burnt umber. The paint has been quite diluted with water, which allows the modelling to be done with light gradations whose brushstrokes are barely visible. Painted by Maria Luisa Vilá.

Painting of FLOWERS

A Painting of Flowers with EXPRESSIVE BRUSHSTROKES

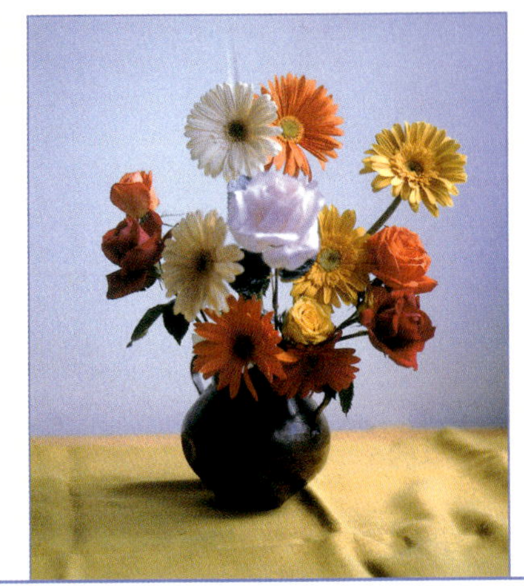

Flowers allow a very free use of colour. A few simple saturated and nervous brushstrokes become colourful fresh flowers. These works let us make use of transparent overlaid colours, the dominance of the gesture and the direction of the brushstrokes. Following this exercise, painted in watercolour, we invite you to create a quick painting with colourful effects.

1

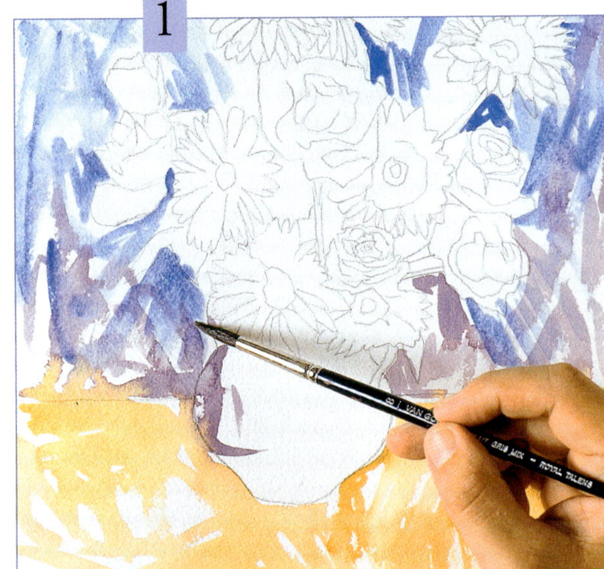

We begin by painting over a previously drawn pencil sketch, since it is easier to work this way. The tablecloth is covered with yellow brushstrokes. Then we almost immediately paint the background with transparent blue and purple washes.

2

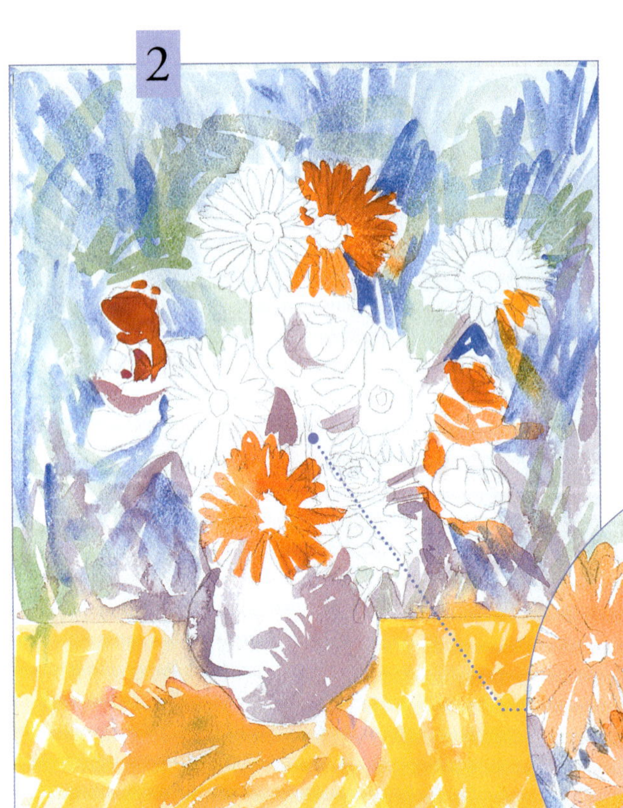

We allow it to dry for a few minutes and then add a few touches of green in the background and magenta on the vase and the shadow it projects. Using orange and cadmium red, we begin to colour the flowers with concentric brushstrokes.

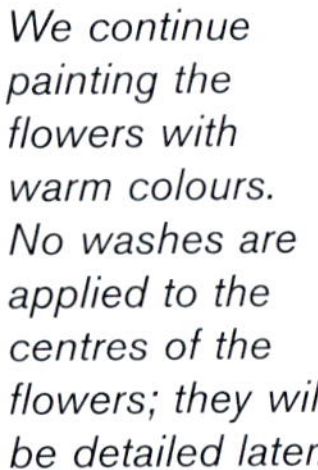

We continue painting the flowers with warm colours. No washes are applied to the centres of the flowers; they will be detailed later.

3

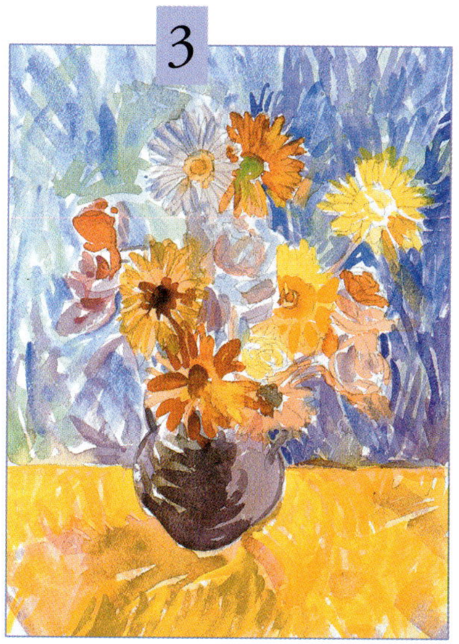

We cover the background with newer applications of blue and violet, and the tablecloth with yellow and ochre washes. The washes of colour applied in several layers create irregular edges and cause some colours to mix with others.

4

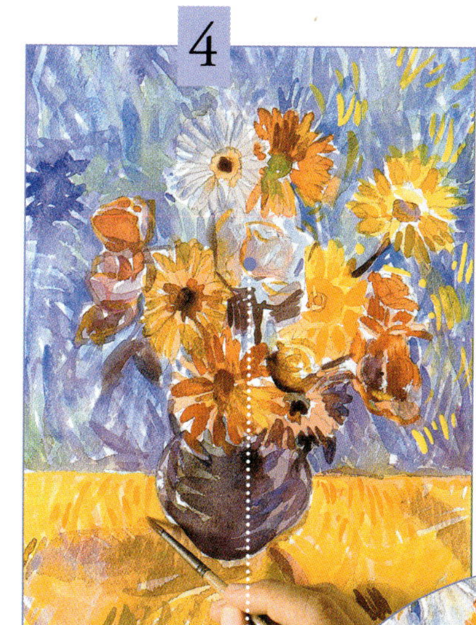

New yellow and orange brushstrokes stand out over the entire surface of the painting, even in the blue background. The short, overlaid brushstrokes of colour in the background and in the flowers vibrate.

5

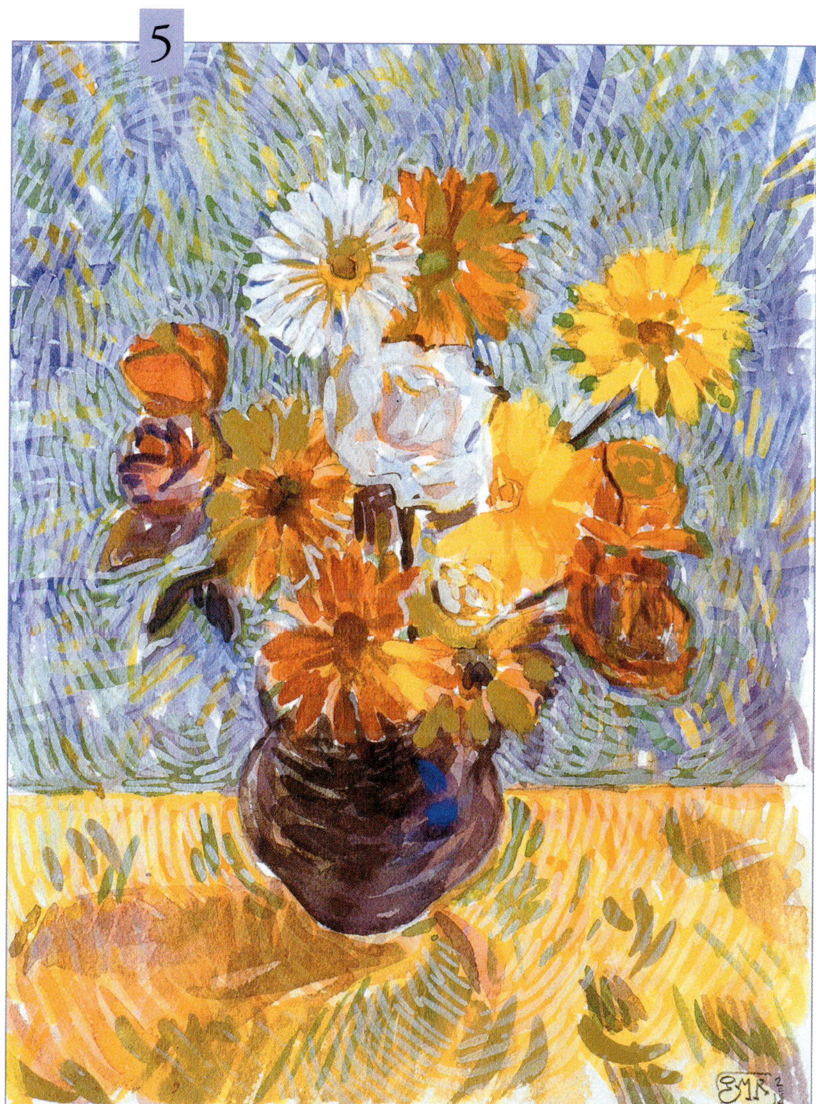

The painting is more and more saturated and dense with flowers and a contrasting background. When the watercolours are dry, we unify the background by overlaying semitransparent brushstrokes of white gouache. The darkest tones give the vase more body and indicate the stems and leaves.

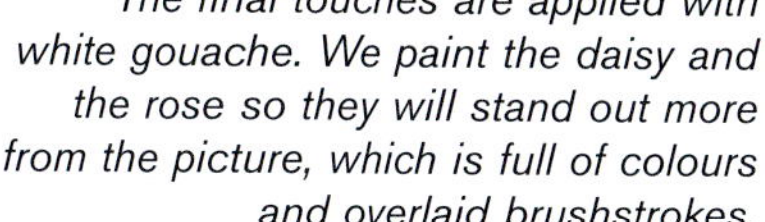

The final touches are applied with white gouache. We paint the daisy and the rose so they will stand out more from the picture, which is full of colours and overlaid brushstrokes.

Tip

The background was covered with thin strokes of white gouache that become more transparent when they dry. They help hold together the large number of brushstrokes in the background and help the bright colours of the flowers stand out.

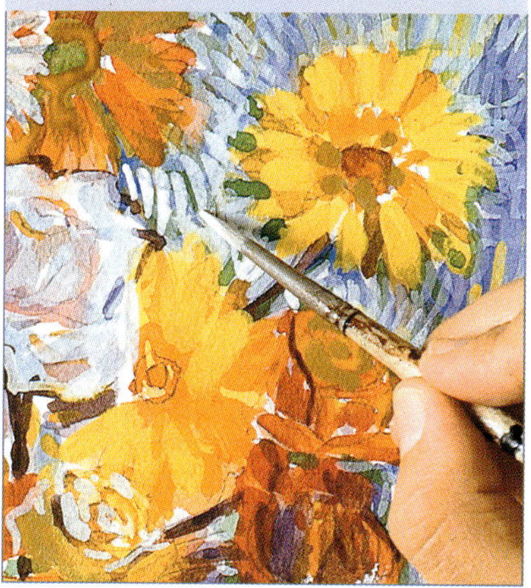

AUGUSTE MACKE *and the Colours of the Tunis School*

Self Portrait by Auguste Macke

The trip taken by Auguste Macke, Paul Klee, and Louis Moillet to Tunis in 1914 turned out to be an important confrontation between Western painting and Eastern painting that years later resulted in the birth of the Tunis School, a group of Arab artists who followed the Colourist style of the European artists.

Macke's interest in Mediterranean colour and Islamic art was aroused by an exhibition he saw at the beginning of the twentieth century in Munich. The artist saw in the East a world of colour replete with fantasy and sensuality. According to the artist, "The image of the Orient allowed a view of a picturesque and colourful world, a passionate and at the same time cruel world, that does not participate at all in the growing disenchantment and the greying of Western civilization." It was a matter of fully embracing colour, and a premeditated rejection of the use of value and chiaroscuro in the Western tradition.

During their trip to Tunis, Klee and Macke abandoned perspective to construct paintings with surfaces covered with complementary colours, thus creating a new pictorial style based on forms that had nothing to do with reality: "Incomprehensible ideas are manifested in comprehensible forms. Comprehensible thanks to our senses, like stars, thunder, flower, like form." Macke focused the interest of his paintings on chromatic structures and the dynamic rhythm of the picture plane. "If you mix red and yellow to make orange, you give the passive and feminine yellow a frenzied and sensual strength, to which blue, the man, is essential. And certainly, blue immediately places itself alongside orange and both colours love each other."

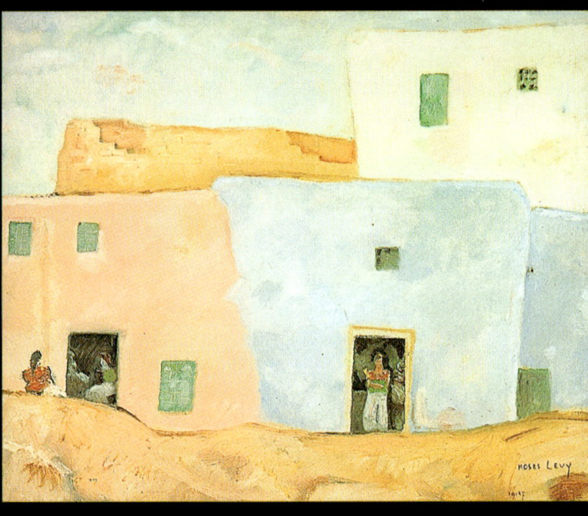

Moses Levy, Hafsia, *1927. Oil on canvas, 18½ × 22 inches (46 × 55 cm) Tunis Ministry of Culture.*

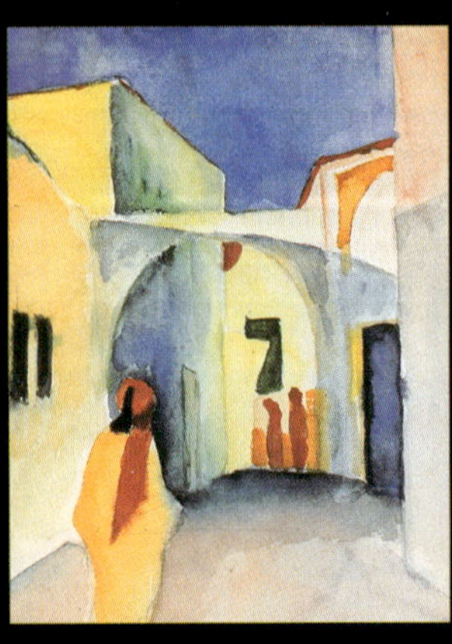

Auguste Macke, View of a Street, *1914. Watercolour, 29 × 22 cm (11½ × 8¾ in), Städtliches Museum of Mülheim.*

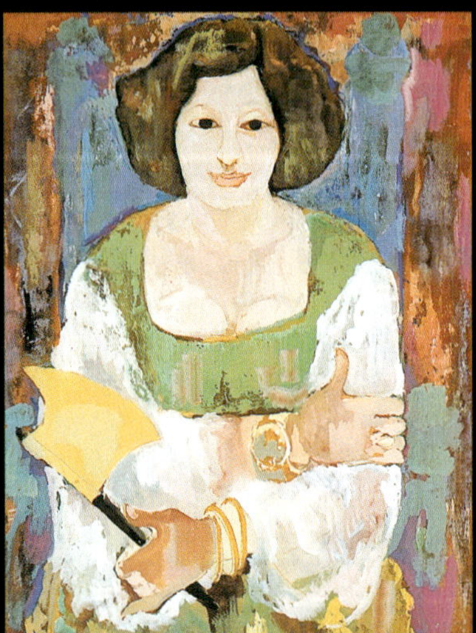

Zubeir Turki, Girl with a Fan. *Gouache and oil, 60 × 40 cm (24 × 16 in), collection of the artist.*

During the 1940s, recovering the spirit of Klee and Macke, a group of amateur and professional Arab painters founded the Tunis School, although many of them had been developing this artistic concept for twenty years. Among them were Zubeir Turki, Hedi Turki, Jallel Ben Abdallah, Moses Levy and Abdelaziz Gorgi.

They praised the light and the beauty of the architecture, the expressiveness of colour and the unique Arabic esthetic. Like Macke and Klee, Moses Levy was taken with Tunisian colour, and through a revitalization of light and colour he was able to strongly and fearlessly express its beauty. The paintings of Zubeir Turki also vibrate with applications of dense and contrasting colour. This artist discovered decoration in the United States, but he remained faithful to the neo-Expressionist figurative painting of the second generation of painters of the Tunis School.